Discovering
GOD'S
Kingdom

More Books in the Series:

Discovering God's Sufficiency
Going beyond ourselves and experiencing the supernatural
Pastoral Health Care — Part One

Discovering God's Love
Confirming God's love through the evidence of historical facts
Pastoral Health Care — Part Two

Discovering God's Counsel
Applying his spiritual solution to meet difficult trials
Pastoral Health Care — Part Three

Discovering God's Heart
Feeling God's heart pulse is our daily challenge
Pastoral Health Care — Part Five

"I have ALS which means that my life is being taken away from me. Don't ask me how I am doing. Every day brings new challenges but I am learning to live each moment with God's presence. I am comforted knowing that the Holy Spirit is traveling each step with me. I ask for his filling every day and even every hour. I am assured of my future with Jesus. As I meditate on his Word, he provides me with his perspective on life — death and all the stuff in between. I will reach my destiny with my team supporters."
— *Cindy Smith*

"I am 100 years old and have all the special physical needs that people my age experience. The spiritual Biblical mediation method works for me. It has strengthened my faith. As I recite the promises, they become a part of my thinking process. My fellowship with God provides natural growth for me both internally and externally. I am thankful that I live with His presence."
— *William Mulder*

"I have grown up with seizures. I know what it is like to lose consciousness. I know my illness is a brain disorder that requires prescribed medicines regularly. Adjusting to the various dosages is a pain. I hate the side effects that I live with. I am enabled through the guidance of the Bible. It keeps reminding me of 'His' nearness. I am thankful for the support I have. I miss my former life and its activities. My prayer is always "keep me close to you, God, and my family!" Discovering God's Sufficiency has challenged me to be close to Jesus Christ."
— *George Odiorne*

"My Life has always looked a little different. I was born with spina bifida and fluid on my brain. I have to live with many side effects like sore back, loss of balance, terrible headaches and short term memory. I have been able to manage every day remembering that God has a purpose for my life. I have been blessed with a family that I need to be here for. Every day brings new challenges that have turned my spirit toward Scripture. To my amazement, God has promised to help me. I can't count the times that I have felt His presence. I know that God has a plan for me and he will accomplish it according to his will."

— *Judy Sharp*

"I have had MS for several years. At the present time, I have been experiencing intense nerve pain. My relationship with Christ has helped me make the adjustments that are needed to survive. I am comforted to know that I will not be stretched beyond my ability to bear. I have confidence that God's will will be accomplished in my life. I have my destiny in heaven where I will experience perfection. I know abiding in Christ is the key."

— *Chuck Boomgard*

"I live with Multiple Sclerosis which is a neurological disease that affects every part of my body. I never know from one day to the next how my body is going to be. I have more MS days than functional days. While losing my worldly independence, I have gained a powerful relationship with my God by choosing to depend upon him. My trust in God empowers me to face every day with joy."

— *Susan Clark Denny*

John's books give us hope and light. He reminds us that through Jesus we are never alone. I have certainly needed that reminder in my life and in my practice. In holding a patient's hand, and helping them through a condition or disease, reminding them that they are never alone has become the greatest gift of health care.

— *Linda M. Kunce, D.C.*

As a Christian who made a commitment to follow Christ as a teen, I have had my share of struggles. In using the book, "Discovering God's Love" it was good to read that Jesus knows what its like to live in a human body. I have received Jesus and His forgiveness, but as the book suggests, I also have power from the Holy Spirit. I should lean on Jesus. Perhaps I can be more secure in meeting the challenges of life. His book encouraged me to gain courage through prayer. The author's honesty is very special to read in this book as he reflects on his own life and struggles. I like his explanation that "the soul is where the emotions are and the mind is where the thinking takes place."

It was good for me to read that God works through weakness, and learn that the author found God with him in the middle of his struggles. My interest was peaked by the questions in Chapter 10. The answers in the book really show why we should follow Jesus. As to love, the book states that God's love is freely given and we show love by touch, words, time and excitement. Quoting Pastor Gillette, I appreciated that he sees life involved in many things, including love. God sees us as His glorious inheritance. Wonderful. Praise God!

—*Arvid W. Vandyke, Ed.D.*

True, illustrative, practical stories are like windows that unlock Bible truths and promises.

Along with masterfully orchestrated short stories should come the truth that God's Word and love has been experienced by His servants as they partner with Him in the work of rebuilding the Kingdom.

Dr. Gillette has done just that in this second book of four relating to life's essential and persistent questions posed to ministers. A gifted teacher, Dr. Gillette lives an ordinary life abiding in Christ and being an obedient servant of the Lord. As he sees God working in his life, and in the lives of those to whom he ministers, his faith is refreshed and he is encouraged to press on through life's uncertainties.

One day, I was "pressing" John for more stories of how he has experienced or seen God's love demonstrated in his own life, and in the lives of his congregants and students. He said to me, "Dr. Mulonge, in pastoring and teaching there are many days, some filled with joy and others marked with pain, that's just life." Thank God for the "all the days" that teach the mighty works, the power and matchless love of God.

Only a lifetime dedicated to nurturing, ministering, teaching, and keen insight through the power of the Holy Spirit, can produce such poignant stories that teach and challenge. Dr. Gillette has done exactly this once again.

—Mulonge M. Kalumbula, Ph.D.

I believe in God's sovereignty and compassion. I am learning to let go of self and to hold onto someone that can do whatever he pleases. Sometimes life is cruel, sometimes it is full of suffering, physically and psychological. A spiritual solution to meet difficult trials has become my goal. God's word carries with it no uncertainties. I want it to saturate my mind and heart.

The *Pastoral Health Care* series was created through unexpected heart disease (open heart surgery), cancer (medication and surgery), a stroke and major head injury after a car accident that also resulted in the death of my wife. I am writing this because it is helping me to develop an adequate level to supernatural, psychological and physiological adjustments. It may help you as well. It has brought me security.

—John F. Gillette, D.Min.

PASTORAL HEALTH CARE PART 4

Discovering GOD'S *Kingdom*

Finding a Way to Understand Ourselves

in a Complex World

JOHN F. GILLETTE
WITH JOY E. GILLETTE
Author of Discovering God's Favor

Chapbook Press

Schuler Books
2660 28th Street SE
Grand Rapids MI 49512

www.schulerbooks.com/chapbook-press

Discovering God's Kingdom: A way to find yourself in a complex world

Copyright ©2016 — John F. Gillette. All rights reserved. Published 2016. Printed at Schuler Books, Chapbook Press, Grand Rapids, Michigan, in the United States of America.

First Edition 2016

Excerpts taken from Discovering God's Presence: A Pastoral Health Care Devotional, © 2015 by Dr. John F. Gillette, D.Min.

Distribution contact:at jjgillette@comcast.net.

ISBN 13: 9781943359516

Library of Congress Control Number: 2016960219

Cover photo: Greg Rakozy/Unsplash
Cover Design: Frank Gutbrod Graphic Design

Printed in the United States of America

The Pastoral Health Care Discovery Series was produced to help during difficult trials in life. It was developed through five volumes.

Adjustments are shared through God's sufficiency. It provides a basic spiritual solution strategy. We have to affirm, accept and adjust to God's plan of action. His superiority, sovereignty and sufficiency will bring victory.

Empowerment is given through God's love. The receiving of his Son Jesus Christ provides power. Historical facts declare the truth.

Enablement is given through God's counsel. Instruction, illumination and application provides the growing process in grace.

Encouragement is given through the awareness of God's kingdom. Learning to accept God's perspective is necessary. The Holy Spirit will travel with us in the present and the future.

Contentment is given through God's heart. The meditation model is the method to follow.

It is with great affection that I dedicate this book series to my wife, Joy, who radiates God's grace. We wrote this Pastoral Health Care Series together.

Applying God's spiritual solutions to meet us in difficult trials has become even more practical in my life with the recent death of my dear wife, Joy. This book has been reproduced in her memory. While the content is the same, my dedication has become more personal than ever before. The separation is painful but as I gather my suffering and feelings of incompleteness, I will succeed with God's peace and presence. The guidelines of this book have brought blessing to our life together. We have pursued them with great persistence. I am assured that she is in God's presence, rejoicing and at peace. I will be with her to experience God's eternal presence someday as well.

"... blessed are they who put their trust in Him."
Psalm 2:12

*This book is lovingly dedicated to
my son John and his wife Sara.
They have discovered God's kingdom through
belief, trust and faith.*

Table of Contents

PART ONE 1

Chapter 1
What Does the Kingdom of Heaven Refer To? *3*

Chapter 2
What is the Promise of Heaven? *5*

Chapter 3
What is the Preparation for Heaven? *7*

Chapter 4
What Will Be Our Participation in Heaven? *9*

Chapter 5
What is God's Perspective on Life, Death and Eternity? *13*

Chapter 6
What Happens When We Die? *16*

Chapter 7
Why Do People Fear Dying? *23*

Chapter 8
When Do We Receive Our Glorified Bodies? *30*

Chapter 9

What Will We Be Like in Heaven? *34*

Chapter 10

Why Do We Call Heaven a "Heavenly Home"? *37*

Chapter 11

What Will Heaven Be Like? *40*

Chapter 12

What Will Get Us into Heaven? *43*

Chapter 13

What Priority Should We Have in the Flesh as We Wait for Heaven? *46*

Chapter 14

What Help is Available to Prepare for Heaven? *51*

Chapter 15

How Do We Practice Love to Prepare for Heaven? *55*

Chapter 16

How Do We Practice Joy and Peace to Prepare for Heaven? *57*

Chapter 17

How Do We Practice Love Characteristics to Prepare for Heaven? *60*

Chapter 18

How Does Transformation Prepare Us for Heaven? *63*

Chapter 19

How Will We Display the Fruit of the Spirit in Heaven? *66*

Chapter 20

Is Heaven Real? *69*

Chapter 21

When is Jesus Coming to Take Us to Heaven? *72*

PART TWO *77*

Chapter 22

What is the Evidence that God Spoke? *78*

Chapter 23

Why Should I Believe? *83*

Chapter 24

What Part Do Angels Have in My Life? *87*

Chapter 25

How Do I Avoid Drifting in My Faith? *91*

Chapter 26

What is My Reliable Resource? *96*

Chapter 27
How Do I Rest in Jesus? *101*

Chapter 28
Who is My Supreme Mediator? *106*

Chapter 29
How Do I Mature in My Faith? *111*

Chapter 30
What Does it Mean to Be a Partaker of the Holy Ghost? *117*

Chapter 31
How Do I Build Relationships? *123*

Chapter 32
What Are Some Promises to Practice in Everyday Living? *126*

Chapter 33
What is Faith? *130*

Chapter 34
Who is Watching Me? *137*

Chapter 35
What is My Heavenly Citizenship Based Upon? *141*

Sources *144*

Acknowledgements *147*

PART ONE

Discovering God's Kingdom deals with life, death, heaven and eternity. It involves a personal decision of belief, trust and faith. Facing death can be fearful. Commitment and knowledge will bring comfort and security. Encouragement will be achieved during the process of death and for loved ones left behind. Allow this book to become your project. Read It as If It Is yours. The questions have been asked by people dying and seeking answers.

What Does the Kingdom of Heaven Refer To?

John the Baptist was the first to preach on this subject. It is based upon spiritual principles which would demand a right relationship with God for entrance into the kingdom. It is a time of preparation for the coming of Christ. The Lord Jesus also preached this message from the very beginning of his ministry. The proclamation of the good news is presented. He sent out the twelve Apostles with the same message. We must be transformed through trusting Jesus Christ in the heart and life to enter the kingdom of heaven.

Righteousness is a requirement to enter heaven. It is not an outward show of self-righteousness. It is not a product of human effort. It is a gift from God.

Jesus was ascended into heaven. The Apostle John was called into heaven. The Apostle Paul was caught up to the third heaven. Stephen the deacon said, "I see the heavens open and the Son of Man standing on the right hand of God" (Acts 7:56). We are going to heaven someday. As you read this, I hope you are preparing for heaven. "Seek ye first the kingdom of God" (Matthew 6:33) on earth and experience the spiritual kingdom. This will lead to preparation for the eternal kingdom, "thy kingdom come" (Matthew 6:10). Heaven preparation comes through seeking God's Kingdom.

2.

What is the Promise of Heaven?

Jesus said, "I go to prepare a place for you" (John 14:2). He is preparing a place for us. When we are absent from the body, we are present with the Lord. Jesus is the way to heaven. The key is "believe in God believe also in me" (John 14:1). "But as many as received him, to them he gave the power to become the sons of God, even to them that believe on his name" (John 1:12). The word 'believe' means to receive, rely upon and trust. We have to have faith in what he said and what he accomplished on the cross. We believe that his death, burial and resurrection have set us free.

Death brings sadness but also satisfaction. It brings eternity into reality. It is a moving day. It will move us out from a temporal body of dust bound by limitations and restrictions. It will someday free us from the sting of death. The body is the earthly house we live in. It is flesh, bones, cells and blood. The soul is my conscience, intellect and will. It includes the emotional life, knowledge I possess and the power of choice. The spirit is the candle of the Lord. It is the breath of God. We are spirit, soul and body. When the spirit leaves the body, it may be difficult at times. As we live in the shadow of the Almighty, the Holy Spirit will lead the way and will bring peace, rest and security. Jesus said, "I will come again and receive you unto myself that where I am there you may be also" (John 14:3). We can have confidence that our physical bodies will be in a state of sleep when our spirit leaves. We know we will then have a spiritual body, "a building made by God" (2 Corinthians 5:1), which will be in Jesus Christ' presence. When he returns, our body, soul and spirit will be united in a resurrected, glorified body. Let us live with this promise as our major focus. Heaven preparation comes through accepting God's promise.

3

What is the Preparation for Heaven?

What should we do to be ready? If we follow the kingdom of God and make our decisions based on eternal values, we will be prepared to enter heaven. As a Christian, we have to learn to live with God's promises activated in our lives. May I share a favorite verse of mine? The scripture says, "Seek ye first the kingdom of God and his righteousness" (Matthew 6:33). The word 'seek' means to choose to follow Jesus with intensity. It will take desire, discipline, determination and devotion. The word 'righteousness' is living out the Christ-like life. It is described in Jesus' own words. He says to be humble. This is an attitude toward ourselves. He says to be repentant. This is an attitude toward sin. He says to be pure. This is an attitude toward the Holy Spirit.

"Kingdom of God' and the 'Kingdom of heaven' refer to the rule of God on earth and the reality of a future kingdom. We can accomplish the preparation process through faith. Faith requires an initiation (God the Father), action (God the Son), conviction (God the Holy Spirit) and commitment (us). The Holy Spirit releases power from inside through our spirit. Allow Jesus to dominate your life. Heaven preparation comes through obeying his word.

4

What Will Be Our Participation in Heaven?

Faith in our lives will produce the fruit of the spirit. The fruit is in a developmental process on earth. It will be continued in heaven without limitations. Love is an attribute of God. He has feeling and affection. The Bible says, "he is love" (I John 4:8,16) and "God so loved" (John 3:16). The love of God has been infused into our hearts through the Holy Spirit. This pre-eminent virtue will express itself in heaven. It will be the fundamental core expressed in our heavenly home. God's grace is seen in his unmerited favor toward us and is produced through his love. Intimacy with God will be unlimited in glory. It all starts here on earth with its limitations. Love is intimacy with God.

Joy is gladness. It is a delight of the mind assured through the goodness of God. Contentment and satisfaction make their appearance in joy. Happiness will follow us into heaven. It is permanent and unspeakable. Joy is enthusiasm in living with strength provided through the Holy Spirit.

Peace is unity. It is a sense of tranquility. It is a restored relationship of harmony with God. Heaven will be full of former peacemakers. It will be a life of peace with God and the peace of God. Peace is a calm and quiet spirit.

Patience is a calm steadfastness. It is respectfulness for one another. In heaven there will be no evil. Submission to God will manifest itself. Life to come will be rewarded with the termination of endurance and longsuffering. There will be no provocation in heaven only the expression of love. Patience is a confident dependence on God.

Gentleness is a quiet spirit. It is always ready to offer assistance. It is a kind heart that will flourish in heaven. It is ready to serve through sensitive desire. It is prepared to decrease personal wishes and to increase Jesus Christ's interest with gentleness. Gentleness is a soft sensitive touch.

Goodness is benevolence. God said, "I will make all my goodness pass before thee" (Exodus 33:19). We have experienced God's supernatural excellence in action. A day doesn't go by when his generosity has not blessed us. Heaven will provide even greater benevolence. Goodness is God knowing our needs and giving what is best for us.

Faith is belief. It is not only an intellectual assent but a reliance on the truth revealed in it. It is the practical submission of the entire man to the guidance and control of such truth. It is the implanted word in us. It is the alignment with God's plan. It is the means to enter heaven and experience his continued faithfulness. Faith is trust in action. It leads to boldness in God's work and brings much heavenly fruit.

Meekness is humility in action. Following God's will reveals meekness. It is the honest understanding of self that presents self in the image of God. It is manifested strength and divine help that builds character. It will continue in heaven with service to the king of the kingdom. Meekness is humble worship.

Godly self-control is spirit-strengthened will-power. It is righteousness in action. Self-discipline will be replaced with uprightness. It is represented by obedience. God's grace has provided the means for victory. Heaven will be a place to glorify God the Father, God the Son and God the Holy Spirit. God is in sovereign control and will reign as our Lord in glory. Heaven preparation comes through demonstrating his fruit.

5

What is God's Perspective on Life, Death and Eternity?

I love the first verse in the Bible, "In the beginning God" (Genesis 1:1). Here we find the first thought to respond to in our question. We have to keep in mind "such knowledge of God is too wonderful for me" (Psalm 139:6). God invites us to know him. We have limitations as human beings. There is also the moral problem and resource issue. He has not revealed everything. He says "Be still and know that I am God" (Psalm 46:10). It starts with "the fear of the Lord is the beginning of wisdom and the knowledge of the Holy One is understanding" (Proverbs 9:10). We may know him through his character. He is distinct from his creation. He is one of a kind. We understand God though his attributes. Do not box him into your little corner. Let God be God. He is self-existent, self-sufficient and eternal. He says, "I am who I am" (Exodus 3:13-14).

God 's perspective on life is found in these words, "The Lord formed man of the dust of the ground and breathed into his nostrils the breath of life and may became a living soul" (Genesis 2:7-9). The body is the material part of man (dust). It is important, valued and honored. It is the temple of God. Life comes from the breath of God and is the non-material part of man (soul). The soul is the part of man that we call personality. It is related to God's image. The soul is related to the body through the brain and is a part of the body. It centers in the mind and makes man unique as individuals. The spirit is that part of human nature that communicates with God. It partakes in some measure of God's own essence. The spirit of man is the candle of the Lord. This may stagger the mind but Gods own breath has caused an inward light.

At death, the body of man goes to the dust and the spirit unto the Lord who gave it. As we face our final destiny, we have to confess that all secular striving is vanity. We should face eternity with confidence and anticipation.

The dictionary defines eternity as perpetual. It is endless without beginning or end. It is not to be confused with mere endless existence which all possess. If we possess only natural life, it will be separated from God. Eternal life will be a life of fellowship with God. We have eternal life with God because we believe in Jesus Christ. The scripture says, "This is the record that God hath given to us eternal life, and this life is in his Son. He that hath the Son hath life and he that hath not the Son of God hath not life. These things have I written unto you that believe in the name of the Son of God, that ye may know that ye have eternal life" (I John 5:11,12). Heaven preparation comes through accepting God's perspective.

6

What Happens When We Die?

May I share my own testimony? I have been told that sometimes if you have experienced open heart surgery, you will become discouraged, doubtful, deceived, discontented, disconnected, distressed, depressed and even feel the threat of death. I can agree because I have traveled that road. I have had an advantage because I have experienced God's greatness, graciousness and goodness through my adventure. I can honestly say that during my heart attack, my fingers were reaching out to Jesus. I had little time to reflect, an urgent cry for help was whispered. With that quick call to a supernatural, sovereign Savior, I was provided with the Holy Spirit's assistance. I have to admit that the Holy Spirit was with me all the way and continues to be present.

I am learning to make the adjustments one step at a time. I have been asked several unhealthy questions, listened to many unwelcomed comments and even some excellent questions and advice have been shared. I live with confidence in Jesus. I was spiritually, psychologically and physically prepared for this journey.

I have experienced a silent heart attack, a severe one and congestive heart failure. What if a third attack arrives on my doorstep and death occurs? The angels will take me immediately to the presence of Jesus. It will be a joyful ride and I am not alone. My earthly body will rest peacefully waiting for my heavenly body. It will be resurrected at Jesus' call. My soul and spirit will be clothed with a building of God. It will experience a sense of well-being and complete satisfaction.

At Jesus' call to come home, I will immediately be in the very presence of the Savior. My fellowship will continue but in a deeper supernatural way. My family will also sense Jesus' promised presence. He will be their comfort in my absence. His love will abound.

His presence will fill the empty seat at the table and conversation. Praise him who is called Jesus.

- Who is this Jesus that I have referred to several times? My relationship and fellowship with him has grown on earth. This continues to be preparation for my heavenly presence with him. The sweet, abundant, intimate and sense of well-being that I have now will only multiply beyond my comprehension when I meet him face to face.

- Who is this Jesus? "Thou shall call his name Jesus; for he shall save his people from their sins." Over seven hundred times in the New Testament this name is used. He is my Savior, protector, provider, leader and Lord. He will never cease his lordship until he has me safe in the sheepfold on the other side. Hallelujah, what a Savior!

- Who is this Jesus? "Behold, a virgin....shall bring forth a son and they shall call his name Emmanuel." 'Immanuel' means 'God with us.' What a wonderful God and Savior is with me. My authority and confidence lies in the fact that Jesus is God. I can rely upon him and be assured that what he says is true.

- Who is this Jesus? "For unto us a child is born, unto us a son is given" (Isaiah 9:6). Seven hundred years before Jesus was born, the prophet Isaiah saw him coming. Isaiah saw that this child was unique. He was "born" and he was "given." In other words, this child was both God and man! As man, he was born and shared in a sinless human nature. As God, he was given, the Father's love gift to a sinful world. This child would be God in human flesh. I am redeemed because his life was a sacrifice for my sins.
- Who is this Jesus? "And the government shall be upon his shoulders"(Isaiah 9:6). In this world, I have turned the government of my life over to him. He has the reins. I have by faith placed the government of my life upon his shoulder. This means that I have surrendered my body as a living sacrifice. It means that I have yielded my mind to him and will continue to learn his truth from his

Word. It also means giving my will to him. I have to add my heart. He reigns at the present time on earth with my body, mind, will and heart. This will continue into heaven. He is supreme.

- Who is this Jesus? His name shall be called Wonderful. Everything about Jesus is wonderful. Whatever he touched took on new substance and new meaning. Today I am able to meditate on his Word and discover his enablement. In heaven I will be able to meditate on him personally. The world is blind. "They seeing see not and hearing they hear not, neither do they understand" (Matthew 13:13). When I was born again, I received a whole new set of spiritual senses. The inner person is raised from the dead and given divine life. My walk with him will walk itself right into eternity. The difference is then I will see with perfect vision, love with a sinless heart and obey with a will that is lost in the glory of God. He makes life wonderful because he is called wonderful.

- Who is this Jesus? "And his name shall be called Counselor." He is my counselor and advisor. He has the right credentials. He is eternal God. He understands. He speaks with love. He encourages, he is patient, he knows me and he prays for me. This counsel prepares me for my journey on earth and my route to his presence and heaven.
- Who is this Jesus? "And his name shall be called the Almighty God." He takes care of the demands of life and hereafter. God has power to meet every need, to handle it, to solve it and to use it for my good and his glory. Since he is God, he deserves my faith, love, obedience, service and worship. To reject Jesus is to reject God and to reject God is to reject life.
- Who is this Jesus? "And his name shall be called the Everlasting Father." He is the originator of eternity. God created me for eternity and Jesus Christ came to earth to reveal eternity. Time and eternity met through Jesus' coming to earth. He is the author of eternal salvation unto all them

that obey him. By the shedding of his blood, he obtained eternal redemption for sins. He has given the gift of eternal life. I am assured of heaven and a touch of his presence now because of who he is.

- Who is this Jesus? "And his name shall be called the Prince of Peace." He provides lasting peace. Poise and a calm confidence in a threatening world of death is promised as the prince of peace gives it. It begins with allowing him to control the government of my life. He reigns here on earth and in heaven. As I seek his righteousness, I will find peace. I may want to change circumstances but the Lord wants to change character. Peace comes to me from the inside out. The more I become like him, the more I will experience peace. Peace will travel with me on my chariot ride to glory. He has been my primary focus on earth and will be the center of my worship in heaven. All I need is Jesus. What about you? Heaven preparation comes through knowing Jesus.

Why Do People Fear Dying?

We can exit from this earth with confidence and leave 'troubled hearts' with hope because our security is in Jesus. We have many favorite Scriptures but this one may be at the top of the list. "Let not your heart be troubled" (John 14:1). This is the foundational statement of the entire chapter. At death, our hearts can be sometimes troubled, disturbed, emotionally drained, confused, lost, sad and restless. Through Jesus' death, resurrection and ascension, we can find rest in knowing the truth. "Ye believe in God, believe also in me." Believing is the key in having a chariot ride to a new address. It is traveling from earth to heaven. It is an exodus and an arrival. If we believe in Jesus, we have access to God the Father. Keep in mind that death was caused by sin. Death is the end of physical life. Death has been swallowed up in victory. Death is a restful sleep for the body.

"In my father's house are many mansions." Death is not a hopeless plunge into the vast unknown. It is an adventure into another level of life. "Absent from the body, present with the Lord." This will take place when I believe that Jesus is the way, the truth and the life. Jesus said, "I am the way to heaven, I am the embodiment of truth" and I am the source of life. To know Christ is to know the Father. To know the Father brings access to heaven. It all begins with the Holy Spirit urging us to respond to Jesus Christ and our decision to respond opens the door of God's heaven for us.

Jesus said, "I go to prepare a place for you. Let your hearts be settled and not troubled. The transition and departure removes the tears from troubled hearts. It will remove fear from the mind. It will remove helplessness from the soul, it will remove hopelessness from the spirit and remove unhappiness from life.

When our soul and spirit are troubled through the death of a loved one, grief is an important and normal response. Whenever a part of life is removed, there is grief. As a follower of Jesus Christ, we take comfort in the certainty of the resurrection. This does not soften the emptiness and pain of being forced to let go of someone we love. Tears, emptiness, loneliness and grief can be understood and strengthened. We know that death is swallowed up in victory. We must learn to live and die in the shadow of the Almighty. Our minds have to believe that Jesus cares for those that have fallen asleep. Our spirits have to believe that death is not the end of existence but the entrance into life eternal. As a matter of fact, the believer "shall never die." Our souls have to mourn. In our reaching inward, outward and upward, the Holy Spirit will give supernatural comfort and peace. These are not glib thoughts. Death is hard. Understanding, reassurance, questions, doubt and analyzing all enter into the aching heart. Encouragement, availability and receptive hearts are a must for this time. Death is universal. As we dwell in the secret place of the most high, we can be comforted as we anticipate seeing Jesus face to face.

I believe if we live under the shadow of the Almighty, we will exit from this world with confidence. May I share some testimonies that represent different levels of spirituality and physical experiences? They all seem to sense a "presence" that gave them peace and a restful spirit. They did not fight to stay alive. Dependence on powers beyond them took over. If we live with a focus on Jesus Christ and live in the reality of his presence, we will die in welcoming his face. This takes daily discipleship. We must learn to take a hold of the hem of Jesus Christ' garment and catch some of the dust from his feet. Growing in grace is Christianity in progress.

As I have shared the thoughts on death, my heart and mind reflected back to several occasions when I witnessed the dying. These testimonies are people that have had the shadow of the Almighty in their life. Fear in the mind, helplessness in the soul, hopelessness in the spirit and unhappiness from life have found a release in discovering security in Jesus Christ.

In the retirement home after many years of living, a mother would wait for God's call home. "I am ready. My body is weak and my mind is forgetting things I should remember. This is a new experience and I am concerned. I believe in the Bible and I have trusted in Jesus to be the resurrection and the life. I am not worried about death and what will happen five minutes later. God's promises have always been true. The journey to death is scary but I have been assured of his presence. My trials will not be beyond me to handle. I walked into her room with tears flowing from my eyes. She was curled up like a little baby with a peacefulness that could be seen in her face. She was now face-to-face with Jesus her Savior. I remember when we were discussing death, we were both reminded that, at the moment the angels would come to escort us up to his presence, he would provide strength, confidence and peace. I took her hand and thanked God for his goodness and mercy.

In the hospital room, I found myself responding to a request to visit a relative of a friend. The friend was concerned for the salvation of the sick relative. The man was not doing well and I was told that he was dying. I was the only one in his room and I was his last visitor. I asked the Lord for help. I was reminded that he was in the Lord's hands. I got close to his ear and mentioned his relative's name. I said I was there to introduce him to Jesus Christ. I had just finished sharing the gospel message and he vomited blood all over. The nurse came in and cleaned him up. I was on a special mission. The patient took my hand, his eyes were closed, he whispered into my ear and took his last breath of air. There was no struggle and there seemed to be a release of his soul to the soul maker. I hope so.

In the hospice care center where he was placed to give him as much comfort as possible, an uncle was lying unconsciously. His life had hidden secrets that came to the surface during his illness and especially now in his dying. Through spiritual sensitivity and discernment, many of the unexpected issues were discussed with concerned people. I learned that he was a believer in Jesus Christ. With that assurance, I proceeded to pray that he would relax in Jesus. I talked about his escort to heaven. He responded by sitting up, smiling and then his heart stopped beating. In his home, a friend shared his death journey with me. He started with agonizing and excruciating pain that ended in the loss of consciousness. The emergency helpers all arrived to assist. His heart stopped. He was blue one minute and the next he was dead. His trip was brief. It was delightful, pleasant, quiet and peaceful. My friend said the death route was awesome and beyond words to describe. He said he did not want to return but the voyage ended with successful resuscitation. He wished he could have remained on the voyage because he never felt such an awesome experience of serenity. Apparently he had something yet to do. He said these encouraging words, "I know one thing, I will not fear death, when God's timing is right, I will take Jesus' hand again and begin the journey." Let us live life with a Christ-conscious intimacy which will bring us to his presence with peace in death. Heaven preparation comes through understanding the truth.

8

When Do We Receive Our Glorified Bodies?

Our earthly body will rest peacefully waiting for our heavenly body. It will be resurrected at Jesus' call. Our soul and spirit will be clothed with a building of God. It will experience a sense of well-being and complete satisfaction.

At death, we go immediately into the very presence of our Savior. Our earthly bodies will become cold and lifeless. It will be put into the grave or it may be cremated. Keep in mind, the body will be raised from the dead. The earthly body is fragile, insecure and will dissolve. We have a building of God and it is solid, secure, certain and permanent. It is heavenly and eternal. The earthly body can enjoy the foretaste of the life everlasting. Transformation is the process that leads to glory. Eternity is not a release into permanent inaction. It is like beginning of action. The heavenly body will find ultimate pleasure and joy in the presence of Jesus. At death, the body goes to the grave but the spirit goes to be with Christ. When Jesus Christ returns for us, he will raise our dead bodies in glory and the body and spirit shall be joined together for a glorious eternity in heaven. Death does not break our relationship with God; it draws us to his very presence. We will be me in heaven, clothed with a spiritual body. Our personalities will survive.

Christ's resurrection provides a final guarantee of the indestructibility of truth. The resurrection provides the fact that good is stronger than evil. It reveals that love is greater than hate. It proves that life is stronger than death. It provides us with a glorified body. We will receive our glorified bodies at the time when our Savior returns to this earth. In the twinkling of an eye all the righteous dead will come forth out of their graves, the soul and spirit will be united.

Our hearts are encouraged and strengthened when we realize that there is an earthly, invisible and glorified body. In understanding this, it brings comfort. "But I would not have you to be ignorant, brethren, concerning them which are asleep, that ye sorrow not, even as others which have no hope" (I Thessalonians 4:13). Our earthly bodies are fragile, insecure and will dissolve. The modern world has investigated the mystery of life and death. Why should we substitute human speculation for divine? We don't have to look for clues. We don't have to wonder about death or life, for we have a revelation from God in his Word. Christ has abolished death. The authority of God's Word gives us the assurance and confidence we need.

The invisible body is the building of God. It is a building not made with hands and is eternal in the heavens. In contrast to the earthly body, it is solid, secure, certain and permanent. The "building of God" is not my heavenly home promised in John 14:1-6. It is eternal, spiritual, beautiful and never will show signs of weakness or decay. Our focus must be on the two words 'we know.' God has told us all we need to know. We know that he is alive;

therefore, we know that death cannot claim us. "Because I live, ye shall live also" (John 14:19). We will receive an invisible body, spiritual in nature, as we enter heaven.

The Bible definition of death is given in James 2:26, "For as the body without the spirit is dead…" At death, the spirit leaves the body and the body goes to sleep and no longer functions. The soul-spirit goes to be with the Lord if the person has trusted Jesus Christ. "Absent from the body and present with the Lord" (2 Corinthians 5:8). When Jesus Christ returns in a moment, in the twinkling of an eye, the glorified body is received at this time. It is like the glorified body of Christ. Our citizenship is in heaven. We expect to see Jesus Christ someday. Our glorified bodies will not be subject to disease, death and decay. It will be fashioned like unto his glorious body. It is conformed to the body of his glory. The resurrection of Christ is the basis of our resurrected body. Heaven preparation comes through his resurrection.

9

What Will We Be Like in Heaven?

The Apostle Paul said that all the righteous would be made alive (the body will be raised). This will take place according to God's order. Jesus Christ is the first fruit, then the righteous dead as well as righteous living and finally the wicked dead will be raised to be judged.

Our bodies in heaven will be like Jesus Christ when he was raised from the dead. This is one of the marvels of God's grace. The earthly body is corruptible. Our heavenly body is glorified. It is flesh-and-bones perfect in every respect. It is beyond our comprehension. Every physical sense will be absolutely perfect. Jesus said, "I am the resurrection and the life; he that believeth in me, though he were dead, yet shall he live, and whosoever liveth and believeth in me shall never die" (John 11:25,26). There is no one fact of history which is better established than the fact that Jesus did actually rise from the dead. Jesus showed himself alive after his death with many infallible proofs.

Our resurrected and glorified bodies require belief in Christs' resurrection. The witnesses were not few but many. Paul's testimony is clear and simple. He declared that he had seen the Lord. The resurrection lies at the basis of apostolic teaching. Our new lives come from the risen Christ. Our new bodies will be a glorious body like his own. The resurrection guarantees a new body. Jesus rose. He died on the cross and in three days he rose from the grave. He appeared to the disciples in his post-resurrection body and walked through the doors they had locked in fear. He said to Thomas, one of his disciples, "put your fingers here, see my hands….stop doubting and believe" (John 20:27). Later Jesus had a fish dinner alongside the Sea of Galilee with his disciples. He performed many miracles.

Our resurrected bodies will be super human. They will be perfect in every way with no weaknesses or limitations. We will be like Jesus. This is breathtaking so use your imagination. The old sin-nature will be forgotten and erased from our memory. Everything that puzzled us in life will be made clear. In heaven, love will be freely given and freely received. The resurrection was proclaimed through God's power. Heaven preparation comes through understanding the resurrection.

Why Do We Call Heaven a "Heavenly Home"?

God's love is the greatest thing in the universe. We didn't appreciate that love in our previous fallen state. We have had to learn some things about him, about ourselves, about creation in God's image, our sin and the revelation of God's wrath against us because of our sin. The only way we can understand his love is through the cross. God's love and the cross came together. Our salvation in Christ Jesus gives us the basis to understand Gods' love and the Holy Spirits' guidance and counsel. Sin bars that realization of his love.

In the Scripture sometimes little two-letter words mean a great deal. In John 3:16, the word 'so' refers to God's great love. It is a love that is infinite. It goes beyond our idea of greatness. It is gracious, sovereign and everlasting. Heaven is heavenly because of God's great love. We have love within us because God indwells us.

God's love is inexhaustible. It cannot be fully understood. How can we understand such love? It is incomprehensible. The challenge is to know the unknowable. The Christian walk is progressive. We need to obtain a deeper knowledge of God daily. We have been touched by this love and yet its fullness lies forever beyond us. Heaven is heavenly because of God's inexhaustible love. We get to experience his unlimited love in heaven.

God's love is a giving love and it is giving the very best. It is the giving of Jesus for our salvation. God has given himself and there is nothing that anyone can give greater than that. Any other gift is insignificant. Heaven is heavenly because of God's love gift. We are getting acquainted with Jesus on earth with its limitations but in heaven, it will be in perfection.

God's love is a sovereign love. It is not influenced by anything in creation. The cause of

God's love is found in himself. His sovereign will dictates his love. He doesn't love us because of us. His love is not regulated by something other than his sovereignty. We are grateful for his love and blessings. We don't deserve it but have accepted it with humility. Heaven is heavenly because of God's sovereign love. The impossible is possible in his sight. We may not comprehend it but through faith we have entrusted our spirit, soul and body to it.

God's love is eternal. It has no end. No enemies, suffering, disaster or anything will separate us from God's love. The supernatural influence and powers are not greater than God. A personal relationship with God through his son, Jesus Christ, is necessary to experience heaven. Heaven preparation comes through love.

What Will Heaven Be Like?

The church was born at Pentecost. It is the beginning of the gospel era. The Holy Spirit will come to indwell us. He is the comforter. He will reprove the world of sin. He will guide us into all truth. He is our divine helper and will lead us into spiritual maturity. The human personality is not of one nature but two (flesh and spirit). The old nature is called the flesh. The new is called spiritual because the Holy Spirit will dominate and control us as we ask for his filling. In our mortal body, we will experience the trials and temptations. Between the two natures, there is constant warfare.

At Pentecost, the ascended Savior poured out the Holy Spirit upon the world without measure. He is here in all his heavenly presence and miracle-working power. Supernatural regeneration produces the fruit of the spirit. Human strength will not do it. Obeying laws, making resolutions, observing rules and reformation will cause failure. Being born again and loving God will bring about the fruit in our lives.

The first condition to walk in the Spirit is to stop resisting the Spirit. We should be in a constant attitude of yieldedness rather than rebellion. This includes the major issues in life and the multitude of small decisions that make up each day. The second condition is to stop sinning against the Spirit. We have a sinful nature. All believers commit sinful acts. God says, "Walk in the spirit and ye shall not fulfil the lust of the flesh" (Galatians 5:16). The third condition is to stop walking in the flesh. This means a moment by moment relationship with the Spirit who dwells within us is necessary. We have received him by faith. We need to have fellowship with him. Faith and fellowship will produce victory.

Our responsibility is to be filled with the Spirit. This means to be constantly dominated by the Spirit. It is not a one grand experience which solves all the problems of the Christian life. Heaven preparation comes through the power of the Holy Spirit. This will be perfected in heaven.

What Will Get Us into Heaven?

I discovered that the Bible is dependable. There are many evidences. The divine genius, the Holy Spirit, has brought them into existence. The way to confident living comes through responding to the Gospel which is the good news that changes your life from the inside out. The Gospel has come to us through the Scriptures. God's Word is the Bible. He says, "I declare unto you the gospel…that Christ died for our sins according to the Scriptures; and that he rose again the third day according to the Scriptures" (I Corinthians 15:1-4).

According to the Scriptures — refers to God's Word, the Bible. Our response to the Scriptures provided a witness within to prove its authority. Acting upon it will provide trust. Jesus is the way, the truth and the life.

'Christ died' refers to the fact that God, the supernatural being who created the heaven and the earth, loved us and gave his Son to die for us. Jesus Christ, the Son of God, became our substitute for the penalty of sin. We have to discover that Jesus solved the problem of penalty of sin, the power of sin and the very presence of sin.

'For our sins' refers to rebellion against God. It is disobedience and a lack of measuring up to his standards. When we believed that Christ carried our sin to the grave and experienced the punishment, we have been forgiven and set free.

'And that he rose again the third day' refers to the proven fact that the sin issue has been taken care of through Christ's death. Through Christ's resurrection, we have power in life to do what God wants us to do. In believing, we have been given a new nature. The Christian life is based primarily upon a decision to entrust ourselves to something or someone. We have to believe what God has to say and to trust Jesus Christ.

Forgiveness, eternal life and full life can be ours. Heaven preparation comes through belief in Jesus Christ and is our passport into heaven.

13

What Priority Should We Have in the Flesh as We Wait for Heaven?

The Bible says, "Knowing this, that our old man is crucified with him, that the body of sin might be destroyed, that henceforth we should not serve sin" (Romans 6:6). Life is full of many struggles. Much of the difficulties stem from the lack of understanding and lack of experiencing true freedom, deliverance and enablement to overcome sin. Do we want to experience the presence of the comforter-counselor in our daily life? He can be a constant companion. The words 'old man' refers to our old self that has died with Christ and the life we now enjoy is a new divinely-given life that is the life of Christ himself. 'The body of sin' refers to our physical weakness and pleasures.

Although the old self is dead, sin retains a foothold in our temporal flesh or unredeemed humanness. 'Might be destroyed' refers to Christ's death and giving us freedom. The sin struggle can be defeated. No longer do we have to lose the battle. What do we mean when we say the 'flesh?' This refers to three designations: the physical body, humanity and the sinful dimension in man. To understand the flesh, we have to have knowledge of the effects of the fall, the character of the sinful nature and how sin manifests itself in our daily life. According to Romans 13:14, the flesh emphasizes a sinful pattern of action. We have to learn to not submit to its demands. The flesh does not refer to the body. The body is not necessarily evil. The body of a Christian is holy, although not yet glorified, and is described as the temple of the Holy Spirit. We can learn to say no to the flesh and wrong thoughts through the power of the indwelling Holy Spirit.

We are able to live the new nature through obeying three valuable lessons. Paul writes the text through the Holy Spirit, the divine genius of the Scriptures. It is based upon the transformation process. The Holy Spirit starts with "I beseech you" (Romans 12:1,2). God is talking to us and telling us that he is our helper and has come alongside of us. We are not alone because the 'therefore' refers to things that have taken place in our life. The word 'brethren' clarifies that we have a relationship with God. This relationship is based upon Christ's death, resurrection, ascension and pentecost. This is Biblical Christianity at its core. Let's think about the divine residence in us, the divine transformation taking place in us and the divine will at work in us.

After Christ came into our hearts through the faith that he had given us, he said 'present' your body, mind and will to me. The word 'present' means a definite decision. It is a once and for all commitment. The words 'mercies of God and reasonable service' gives us the reasons that are logical for us to give our total life to him. He says, 'present your body a living sacrifice, holy, acceptable.' We have to recognize the divine residence in our bodies. A change has taken place because now we are a new person. Do we realize that the God we love through Jesus Christ is dwelling in our very being and are we living it out for all to see?

The next part of the text shows us how to live out the divine presence. "Be not conformed to this world but be ye transformed by the renewing of your mind" (Romans 12:2). We must respond to the divine transformation. We manifest God's redemption through our redeemed nature. The Holy Spirit releases power from inside through the spirit. This takes place when we allow Jesus Christ to dominate our life through the saturation of his Word in our minds. We have to learn that in everything Christ must be the focus.

The third section of the text says, 'That ye may prove what is that good and acceptable and perfect will of God.' God is working his will in us. He is shaping us into the image of Christ. The divine will is at work in us. It all depends on what or who we put our faith in. Faith requires an initiating action and commitment. We have to respond to God's demands and be undergirded by love. Have we learned that each day belongs to him? His will is that we yield our agenda for the day to him and let him work it as he sees best. His will is that we understand that the mind controls the body and the will controls the mind. His prayer is "Thy will be done" (Matthew 6:10). Heaven preparation comes through walking in the Spirit.

14

What Help is Available to Prepare for Heaven?

The Bible says, "In whom ye also are built together for an habitation of God through the Spirit" (Ephesians 2:21-22). "Know ye not that ye are the temple of God and the Spirit of God dwelleth in you? If any man defile the temple of God, him shall God destroy; for the temple of God is holy, which temple ye are" (I Corinthians 3:16-18). It may be a shock but God the Holy Spirit indwells us. The glory of the church is the glory of the presence of God and that glory came at Pentecost. Jesus made the promise, "The comforter will come, even the spirit of truth, whom the world cannot receive, because it seeth him not, neither knoweth him but ye know him; for he dwelleth with you and shall be in you" (John 14:17). The Holy Spirit has to convict us regarding sin and salvation. Salvation comes through our belief in Christ's death and resurrection for the forgiveness of sin. The reception of Jesus Christ in the heart brings the residence of the Holy Spirit.

The Holy Spirit will never be withdrawn from us. We may grieve the Holy Spirit, we may hurt him, we may refuse his guidance and we may reject his wisdom, but he will never be withdrawn from us. Once he comes into our hearts, he abides there forever. We will never be disowned by him even if we are disobedient and fruitless. It has been said that the Father is the originator, the Son the executor and the Holy Spirit is the applicator. In salvation, for example, the Father gave his Son, the Son came to pay the price for sin and break the power of death and the Holy Spirit applies the salvation that has been provided. The Holy Spirit does the convicting. He has helped us to recognize our helpless and lost condition. He has caused our hearts to place trust in Christ for salvation. Let us not evade the truth. We cannot make our own definition of sin. We cannot establish our own standard of righteousness. We cannot formulate our own idea about judgment. We must give heed to him as he points us to the Lord Jesus Christ.

He not only convicts and regenerates our soul but through Christ, we are baptized in the Holy Spirit. At the moment of salvation, we experienced spirit baptism and were placed in the body of Christ, the church. He helps us to deal with the flesh problem. He intercedes for us. He offers prayer on our behalf. He rescues us and knows exactly what is best for us. He knows the overall plan. He anoints and illuminates the Word of God. No deception of the enemy will cause us to go astray. He also fills me (Ephesians 5:18). To live the Christian life means to live in the power and under the guidance of the Spirit of God. No longer do we have to give in to our natural inclinations. To be filled with the Holy Spirit means we are completely under his control.

How do we live with that filling? We have to daily trust the Lord and obey his word. We look to him for his strength and enablement. We believe in his promises and obey his commands given in the Bible. When we fail, and we will, we must confess the sin and claim the forgiveness and cleansing. The Holy Spirit will increase his presence as we dedicate ourselves to do his will in an attitude of humanity and submission. He is in control. Heaven preparation comes through the indwelling of the Holy Spirit.

15

How Do We Practice Love to Prepare for Heaven?

Love is a product of the ministry of the Holy Spirit. It is fused into us by his supernatural power. We have love because God indwells us. We have to make a decision to love. It involves action. It is a command to obey. It should be our priority. When God says heart, soul and mind, they refer to completeness. It is a virtue to be sought above all others. God the Father is our example. He 'so loved' means he gave the ultimate gift. We have to choose to love, to maintain the action of love and to ensure that the product of love Is genuine. If we do not love, we are not genuine. The transforming power of the Holy Spirit has to take place. The words 'inward, within and inner' all refer to the union we have with Christ. The inner witness will flow outwardly, not because of self-effort, but because we love God with intensity.

Love will establish our fellowship with God. If our love is in the right condition toward God, obedience to his word will be welcomed. Rejection will bring the absence of the Holy Spirits' power. Love requires service. The word 'but' in this text means contrast. The old nature can be conquered. The impulse to do evil can be changed. Our freedom is not for selfish fulfillment but for serving others. Heaven preparation comes through love which involves indwelling, action, obedience, sacrifice, intensity and fellowship.

16

How Do We Practice Joy and Peace to Prepare for Heaven?

The Bible says, "Now the God of hope fill you with all joy and peace in believing that ye may abound in hope through the power of the Holy Ghost" (Romans 15:13). As the indwelling comforter-counselor produces love in us for God and our neighbor, we are able to experience joy and peace. Keep in mind the confident words 'now the God of hope,' because they give security, strength and steadfastness. Hope is not wishful thinking but confident expectation or anticipation. We have to accept the truth that God wants us to have his joy and peace. We must believe him and we must choose to receive his divine provision and refuse all that hinders our life of joy and peace.

This joy is rejoicing in spite of suffering and adverse circumstances. Persecution will arrive on the doorstep of believers. Warfare is a constant reminder of the battle for truth. Heaviness of heart will be for a season. Various trials will come but our sovereign God is in charge and knows what we can bear. As we trust and rely on the Holy Spirit, the genuineness of our faith will be bright. As we abide in Christ, we will experience a shared divine joy. We have to only remind ourselves that joy is related to obedience, abiding, prayer, truth, hope, faith, believing and the Scriptures. We can achieve it through salvation, fellowship, worship, the work of Jesus Christ, the work of the Holy Spirit, the ministry to others and the decision to choose to receive joy in obedience and faith.

The text refers to not only joy but peace. This power is based upon a relationship with God and his grace. We have been justified by God. This is not the peace of God but peace with God. This is not a feeling of peace but a state of peace. Jesus Christ has become our mediator. It is through his blood. Peace with God will provide the peace of God. Peace with God is dependent upon faith and peace of God is dependent upon prayer. Peace is provided through the atonement of Jesus Christ. It is found in the victory of Jesus Christ. It is found in the work of the Holy Spirit. We are to "let the peace of God rule in my heart" (Colossians 3:15).

It is the peace and tranquility of heart that he left as a legacy to his disciples. The word 'rule' is important because it becomes the umpire. Wherever there is a conflict of motives or impulses or reasons, the peace of Christ must step in and decide which is to prevail. The Holy Spirit helps to make the adjustments. The word of Christ must be at home in our being which should have unrestricted liberty in our lives. A knowledge of it is necessary. 'Admonish' is an outcome of the knowledge and wisdom. It provides encouragement and reproof. Whatever we do, we want to do it heartily as to the Lord.

Heaven preparation comes through practicing joy and peace.

17

How Do We Practice God's Love Characteristics to Prepare for Heaven?

Longsuffering, gentleness and goodness are the characteristics of the action of love. The fleshly pattern of envy, anger, jealousy and hostility must be nailed to the cross. The choice has to be made. It is a decision to depend upon God to express love.

The expression of patience is released by the comforter counselor. This is possible and absolutely necessary.

Discover the great promise that says, "strengthened with all might, according to his glorious power, unto all patience and longsuffering with joyfulness" (Colossians 1:11). We are empowered with all power. The spiritual power comes from God. We are reminded of his limitless power. It is given according to his abundant supply. We can try as hard as we want and patience will fail. It is not based upon our strength but rather our desire and willingness to abide in Jesus Christ. Consider the three words 'strong, power, might.' We can find the Divine Trinity within these words. They give us a sense of security and confidence.

Patience is the capacity to see things through. It is described with fortitude and endurance. Longsuffering is self-restraint. This characteristic is produced through the practice of lowliness which is the attitude of exaltation directed toward Jesus Christ, not self. It is humility in action. It is living with the sense of awe toward God. Meekness is submission to God's will and gentleness toward men. Love integrates it all together. The light of Jesus and the radiance of his person can be in our lives. When we experience the radiance of Jesus in our life. we can live in a sense of awe toward God. When we realize that God is more than the sum total of his attributes and try to contemplate his person, we will be able to rest in him. Waiting to respond with love with which he infuses us will be a possibility. Heaven preparation comes through the action characteristics of love.

How Does Transformation Prepare Us for Heaven?

The Bible says "Likewise reckon ye also yourselves to be dead indeed unto sin, but alive unto God through Jesus Christ our Lord" (Romans 6:11). Jesus Christ died on the cross to set us free from our selfishness, pride and bondage. We have to learn daily to nail these sins to the cross and receive the ministry of the Holy Spirit so we may be characterized by a transformed life which involves faithfulness, meekness and self-control. The Holy Spirit is intimately involved in this work of transformation in our lives. He seeks to work in us so that we may experience love, joy and peace. In relationships, he provides the expression of gentleness and goodness. His goal for us is to be faithful, meek and to exemplify self-control.

The fall caused the effect of alienation. This has produced rejection, inferiority, anxiety, hostility, fear, inability and weakness. Redemption has caused reconciliation to God. Guilt, unrighteousness, bondage and death have been taken care of. Now we are being conformed to the image of the Lord Jesus. Growing will take place as we learn and practice the truths of the Scriptures. Faithfulness is a work of transformation. Faithfulness means that I am reliable and trustworthy. It refers to commitment to the 'Word.' Hold to it, keep to it, continue in it and pattern it in life. Dependence and intensity go hand-in-hand to win a crown of life.

Meekness is a mark of transformation. Walking worthily requires submission to God's will and gentleness toward men. Meekness is not weakness but a delicate consideration for others. Meekness is having knowledge, boldness, reverence and worship toward God, not fear. Meekness is possible through the engrafted word and being a doer of the Word. The Scriptures have been implanted in us through submissiveness.

It has to be practiced continually. Meekness is manifested in life through the obedience of the Word. A perfect example of meekness is found in the life of Christ.

Self-control is a characteristic of transformation. It is rational restraint of the natural impulses. The only way we can be in control is through the power of the divine. This takes place as we apply his promise to everyday activities The Christian is indwelt by the spirit of God. He has become our divine helper and will lead us into spiritual maturity. We have to honor the presence of the Holy Spirit and aggressively cooperate with him. Our sinful tendencies in this area of pretense must be confessed. The Holy Spirit's goal is to glorify Jesus Christ. We are able to accomplish his goal through daily surrender and daily cooperation. Heaven preparation comes through transformation.

19

How Will We Display the Fruit of the Spirit in Heaven?

It is interesting to know that the fruit of the spirit expressed in our daily activities will equip us for heaven. The fruit is produced through abiding in the vine, Jesus Christ. The supernatural fruit is preparation for heaven where it will be experienced without limitations. The character of Christ will be revealed in us. It all starts with being rooted and grounded in Christ. Our personality will be Christ-like. Living in the flesh is life without God. Life with God is living in the spirit. We are powerless without Christ. Christ lives his life through us. The reality of this fact takes place in its fullness in heaven.

- Heaven will be a place of peace. It is a place of sweetness — no cosmetics for sweetness

but the real thing. We will be present with the peacemaker.
- Heaven will be a place of warmth. Gentleness is the attitude of pleasantness. We will experience God's gentle and quiet spirit.
- Heaven will be a place of generosity. It is a place of supernatural work. We will experience God's goodness.
- Heaven will be a place with no provocations. It's a place without aggravating circumstances. We will experience patience.
- Heaven will be a place of sovereign control. It's a place of grace fused together with strength, gentleness and meekness.
- Heaven will be a place of spirit-strengthened will-power. Righteousness will shine through. Self-discipline will be replaced with uprightness.
- Heaven will be a place of love and thankful hearts to Jesus for the ransom he paid, a love fused by God the Father and translated to one another.

- Heaven is a place of joy. It's a divine happiness that undergirds all emotional reactions. It's a life of enthusiasm and beauty.
- Heaven is a place of obedience. It's a trust in God that started on earth. It's an alignment with his Word. The connecting factor is faith.
- Heaven is a place that will characterize the qualities of Jesus Christ. Fellowship with him will last forever. God's unmerited favor has taken place.

Jesus said, "Let not your heart be troubled… believe in me" (John 14:1). We are known by him and we can know him. The focus is on him. This is what makes heaven real. Heaven preparation comes through demonstrating the fruit.

Is Heaven Real?

Writing about dying and heaven will bring many questions to mind. What does the Bible say about the golden streets and the pearly gates? What is dying like? Is heaven a real place? Does dying bring suffering? Will our exit from earth be pleasant? Are the angels our escort team? Is heaven visionary? Is it just a big dream? What will unconsciousness be like? Can we believe the testimony of people that have died and visited heaven and returned? What is it like to really know God? What is the eternal life? The priority is to know God. Life is not a bad joke. It is not a dreamy idea. In knowing God, life will bring about the answer that we are searching for. To know Jesus is to be saved by Jesus, here and hereafter, from sin and guilt and death. Knowing Jesus is knowing God. Knowing

God is a personal involvement in mind, will and feeling. Knowing God is a sovereign grace word, pointing to God's initiative in loving, choosing, redeeming, calling and preserving. The main idea is that God knows us. Our earthly journey and heavenly destiny is found in knowing God.

Discovering God's presence will compel us to stand out against evil and the dictates of this world. The Kingdom of God will make us stand firm and take action. Our eternal destiny will energize us. Knowing God will prepare us for heaven and our departure from earth. Praying is the source of strength. It will bring us into direct contact with the heavenly Father which ultimately will bring us into his actual presence.

His presence will provide confidence, "the Holy God is in thee" (Daniel 4:18). God's hand is on history at every point. The unfolding of his eternal plan and the kingdom which will triumph in the end is God's. Our thoughts are challenged with the understanding that he knows our destiny. His kingdom and righteousness will triumph. "Blessed be the name of God forever"

(Daniel 2:20). We will be brought into His Majesty's presence. His gracious faithfulness will be the driving force that will result in heaven.

Peace and assurance will be guaranteed. A calm contentment even in the midst of a burning fiery furnace is promised. There is no panic, no worry, no anxiety and no concern. We belong to the Lord Jesus Christ. Heaven preparation comes through confidence.

When is Jesus Coming to Take Us to Heaven?

Read the headlines:
- Cyclone causes thousands of deaths
- Powerful volcano erupts
- Widespread epidemic
- Russia is resurging
- America is in an economic tailspin
- Widespread hunger
- Global conflict
- Fear and anxiety is everywhere
- National political issues

The questions we cannot ignore are:
- Why is Israel so important?
- Who controls the world's oil supply?
- What is the European Unification?
- Who does Islam hope to rule?

- What is causing America to decline?
- What is a profile of the coming World Ruler?
- Will there be a Russian, Islamic invasion of Israel?
- What does the Battle of Armageddon refer to?
- What is God's sovereign plan?

We believe in the imminent return of Christ. "In a moment, in a twinkling of an eye… we shall be changed" (I Corinthians 15:52). "We shall be caught up to meet the Lord in the air" (I Thessalonians 4:16,17). We are gathering together to meet him.

A conscious awareness of his sudden return prepares us to be ready. It may seem strange but to be raptured, snatched or translated from this earth is not a new experience. It may be in our next breath of air. It may be the next blink of our eye. It may be our next heartbeat. It may be our next sign that the Lord could descend from heaven with a shout and call us home. It has already occurred three times. "Enoch walked with God; and he was not, for God took him"

(Genesis 5:24). The New Testament adds, "By faith Enoch was translated so that he did not see death and was not found because God had taken him; for before his translation he had this testimony that he pleased God" (Hebrews 11:5). "Elijah went up by a whirlwind into heaven" (2 Kings 2:11). After Christ's resurrection, he ascended into heaven. "They watched and he was taken up and a cloud received him out of their sight…he will come in like manner as you see him go into heaven" (Acts 1:9-11).

All of these events describe a natural body of flesh being changed and translated into the presence of God. Jesus Christ will do the raising. This unique event is for believers. Belief is the key. Believing, relying, accepting and confessing the truth of the gospel is the answer. Now we are waiting, "wait for his Son from heaven whom he raised from the dead, even Jesus who delivers us from wrath to come (I Thessalonians 1:10; 5:9). This is the order of events for our translation:

- The Lord himself will descend
- He will shout as he descends

- The dead in Christ will rise
- The living in Christ will be changed
- A reunion of believers will take place in the clouds
- The judgment seat of Christ will take place
- Christ's return will take place

The Bible says, "Knowing the time, that now it is high time to awake out of sleep; for now our salvation is nearer than we first believed" (Romans 13:11). What is happening at the present time will not continue indefinitely. Christ will set things right. We have to learn to wait, work and watch. Life is short. We have to remember our roots are built upon eternity. We may be fragile and vulnerable in the flesh but strong and powerful in the spirit. The warning signs in Matthew 24-25 will intensify. All the prophecies related to Christ's glorious appearing will take place. The translation of the church takes place seven years before his glorious appearing

Both events appear in Titus 2:13; the blessed hope (rapture-I Thessalonians 4:13-18) and the glorious appearing (second coming-II Thessalonians 1-2). More importantly, we claim the words "the great God and our Savior Jesus Christ are one." This is a strong statement of the deity of Christ. Whatever happens, he is in charge. We will be translated into his presence and will return with him. Heaven preparation comes through believing the prophecies.

PART TWO

In writing 'Discovering God's Kingdom, I was reminded of James 4:8, "Draw nigh to God and he will draw nigh to you." Spirituality involves regeneration and submission. I have looked at the basic questions asked by interested people. Part Two involves my personal encounter in answering the question, How do I draw near to God and how does he draw near to me? It has brought peace to my soul. I hope it will do the same for you.

22

What is the Evidence that God Spoke?

How do I draw near to Jesus to prepare for heaven? It is through accepting the authority of Jesus. The Bible says, "God, after he spoke long ago to the fathers in the prophets in many portions and in many ways, in these last days has spoken to us in his Son" (Hebrews 1:1,2). The best way I can know God is through him talking to me. I am thankful for the evidence that he spoke.

Look at the world around you. It is a reminder of God's wisdom and power. In Job 38, it declares an observation of nature. He says look at creation. I made it. "The heavens declare the glory of God; and the firmament shows his handiwork..." (Psalm 19:1-4). In recent years,

I have had several surgeries. In them I have discovered that an intelligent designer had to be behind the complexities that involve my body. The surgeries have been involved with the most important organ, the heart, down to the smallest. The body and universe are a source of theology. God speaks through nature and humanhood.

The Bible is the voice of God. Men were used, their minds were used and their personalities, but God totally controlled them by the Spirit. For me to know anything about God, he must tell me. He prepared me to listen to his voice through the Holy Scriptures. He provides the understanding. Believing the supernatural is not through the natural. It is developed through the supernatural. Evidence is found in his words "to the fathers, in the prophets, in many portions — many ways…" The prophets are his messengers. A prophet is one who speaks to men for God. They are commissioned by God (2 Peter 2:21; 2 Timothy 3:16). Many portions refer to the written words. Discover the thread that connects them all (Jesus Christ). The many ways emphasize the many literacy ways, narrative, poetry, law, prophecy, doctrinal, ethical and moral. Through the inspiration of his Spirit, he caused certain men to write down a series of documents that we call the Bible. God has specifically revealed himself through the words of Scriptures. The way to get familiar with the mind of God is through reading his Word. The book is unique. It is a carefully orchestrated collection of documents that have been accurately and amazingly preserved for thousands of years. It has been miraculously conceived and safeguarded. He not only speaks through nature but he communicates through his revelation (Ezekiel 1:1-3; Zephaniah 1:1). His existence, nature, will and love are revealed.

Evidence is found in the fact that God has spoken to me in "his Son." From beginning to end, the New Testament is Christ. The Old Testament was given in bits, pieces and fragments. Jesus Christ is God's full and final revelation. God has fully expressed himself in Christ. Jesus Christ is identified as the Creator of all things (John 1:1-3). He is the originator of all creation and communication. His personality and character give evidence of his deity (John 14:9). He is the "begotten Son" of God (John 1:18). The ultimate revelation of God is Jesus Christ (Hebrews 1:1,2). "Christ came, who is over all, the eternally blessed God" (Romans 9:5). Evidence is promised through my acceptance of Jesus Christ as Savior and authority is given through the Holy Spirit's illumination to my mind and heart. The evidence that God spoke is written into my heart through his creative ability, through his written word and through his complete revelation Jesus Christ. This has caused an imprint on my innermost being. Without Christ, I possessed an inner knowledge of God (Romans 1:18-32). He has implanted in my heart this idea. In Jesus Christ, I have the indwelling Holy Spirit to bear witness of the truth (John 14:26). My conscience bears witness (John 14:107).

Evidence that "God spoke" comes from within my spirit. I have shared in my spiritual autobiography, "Discovering God's Favor" several evidences of the authority of the Bible. As I reflect upon evidences, the Holy Spirit has produced an impression on my spirit and soul that it is true. He is the agent of influence. My intellect, feelings and senses have become aware of his internal presence which provides an external conviction. This reflection has made me recite the truth. I have been indoctrinated with the truth. This has developed an understanding and complete reliance. Every day I have been reminded that the Scriptures work when I apply it to my daily activities. The reflecting, reciting and relying has brought restoration. Deliverance, boldness, confidence and peace have resulted in a restful spirit. The absolute truth of the reality of the Bible has brought the end product of rest in Jesus Christ.

Why Should I Believe?

How do I draw near to Jesus to prepare for heaven? It is through accepting the deity of Jesus. "In these last days (God) has spoken to us in his Son" (Hebrews 1:2,3). I have believed and committed my life to Jesus Christ because he has been appointed heir of all things. Everything is under the control of Jesus Christ. All that God possesses; Jesus Christ possesses (Psalm 2:6,7). He created all things. He is Lord and Christ (Acts 2:36). I belong to his kingdom so therefore, I am Jesus Christ's heir (Romans 8:16,17). I have believed and committed my life to Jesus Christ because he created all things. Christ is the agent through whom God created all things. He created everything material and everything spiritual. He has created time, space, energy and matter. The Bible tells me that Jesus Christ made the universe.

I have believed and committed my life to Jesus Christ because of his radiance. This word represents Jesus as the manifestation of God. I cannot see God but his presence is seen in Jesus Christ. Jesus is the light of life (John 8:12). He is the radiance of God's glory. The glory of God is found in his nature, character, power and acts. Christ is the very representation of the divine essence. The phrase expresses the fact that the Son of God is a distinct person from the Father and yet one with him in the Godhead. His light gives me life. His radiance (light) gives me purpose, meaning, happiness, peace, joy, fellowship and everything for all eternity. I have believed and committed my life to Jesus Christ because of his being.

Jesus Christ is the express image of God. He was God in substance. He is the exact reproduction of God (Colossians 2:9). He is God's equal. His inner nature, essence and substance are the same. He is deity. I have believed and committed my life to Jesus Christ because of his administration. He sustains all things by his word and that word has a divine power. The word "uphold" means to support and to maintain. It means continuous action. Christ's pre-eminent power monitors the universe. Things do not happen by accident. I have believed and committed my life to Jesus Christ because of his sacrifice. Jesus Christ paid the penalty for my sin. When I accept his death and believe that he died for me, I am set free and purified from the stain of sin (I Peter 1:18,19). "The blood of Jesus…cleanses me from all sin" (I John 1:7). This takes place through faith. I believe and I committed my life to Jesus Christ because of his exaltation. Jesus sits at the right hand of God. This shows that he accomplished what he set out to do. His sacrifice is sufficient. He offered one sacrifice and said "it is finished." I am thankful for the reasons why I believe and am assured of his intercession on my behalf (Romans 8:34). The pre-eminent Christ is prophet, priest and king.

As a young child, it was easy to believe in Jesus Christ. I was taught all the stories about Jesus. They were interesting and convincing. In simple trust, I believed. Later in life those same stories were a part of my thought pattern. They became deeper in their meaning. I reflected on the true radiance of Christ. In reciting that reflection, it developed understanding. It is easy to trust in Jesus Christ when you discover that in his radiance, he is God. Reliance becomes a pattern for life. As it increases, restoration and deliverance from doubt occurs. Having rest in Christ every day is the end product of faith.

24

What Part Do Angels Have in My Life?

How do I draw near to Jesus to prepare for heaven? It is through accepting the superiority of Jesus. "Let all the angels of God worship him" (Hebrews 2:4-14). They are holy, powerful and wise. They are specially created spirit beings made by God before he made man. There are 108 direct references to angels in the Old Testament and 165 in the New Testament. The primary purpose for their creation was to render special worship and services to God. Angels are spirit- beings and do not have flesh and bones, but they do have bodies. They can appear in human form. They minister to Christ and his church. They assist God in answering prayer, giving deliverance from danger, giving encouragement and protecting children.

Early in my ministry, I believe I had an encounter with angels. My wife and I were traveling to a speaking engagement and we were excited about this preaching event. I enjoyed preaching and was energized to share what I have learned from the Scriptures. It was in the dead of winter and the weather was very bad with 6 foot drifts of snow. I could hardly see where I was going. For a moment I thought no one would come out in this condition. The pavement was pure ice and I thought I should call the church and return home, but I really wanted to minister. The conditions became so bad I had to crawl along at the speed of a turtle. I began to pray for protection and confidence that we were doing the right thing. Suddenly my car started to slide toward an embankment. I was out of control of the car. I grabbed my wife, prayed urgently to Jesus — "help, help, help!" In moments we could see our history before us. It seemed like a movie and we were the major focus. There was nothing I could do. The car was going to roll over down that steep embankment. We landed in the medium.

People came to help from many directions. Our triple call for help was already answered. Someone else had taken over the driving and kept us safe. I think it was a guardian angel. It is hard to believe but we made it to the church on time, had a big attendance with great results in the service. The Lord was glorified.

Since that time I have made a special study of angels in my doctrinal digest series that ended up being a part of my research doctorate field project. Other experiences have appeared to provide further confidence. We prayed to God the Father, through his Son and with the guidance of the Holy Spirit and protection was granted. I have had other interventions as well. Praise to Jesus who is over the angels and dominates my life. Jesus is better than angels in five ways, in his titles, his worship, his nature, his existence and his destiny. Jesus is superior in everything. He was responsible for providing safety and the angels served on his behalf.

I have reflected upon angels many times. It seems that I have had several encounters with them without knowing it. I was on my way to a preaching engagement and lost my way. I did not have any electronic equipment to guide me. I looked at my watch and realized that I was going to be late or even miss the service. I drove to the side of the road and began to pray in deep earnest. Please, Lord, help me to find my way. I was out in the country with corn fields, cows and no houses or people nearby. What am I going to do? I could not even get a sense of direction and was running out of time. Then out of nowhere, somebody came walking up to the car and said, "it looks like you need some help." I told him my dilemma and he said, "that is why I am here. You are only a few miles from your destination. You will make it on time to serve your master." I looked back but could not see the person that helped me. He could have been an angel. Notice that he said we are serving the same master. In my reflection, I have recited my experience many times. This practice has brought complete relief. Renewal and rest have been the end product in my life.

How Do I Avoid Drifting in My Faith?

How do I draw near to Jesus to prepare for heaven? It is through accepting Jesus' abiding presence. "...We must pay much closer attention to what we have heard lest we drift away from it" (Hebrews 2:1). Christ is anointed above all others, the Lord of creation, the unchangeable, everlasting God (v. 8-12). I cannot allow what I have heard about him to slide through my mind. I cannot be careless in my efforts to follow Jesus. Sometimes it is not a deliberate desire. It is just a slow process that made me slip. This is how to avoid the drifting process. I have to make the Word of God my own. A personal commitment is necessary.

I have met a lot of people that have lost the way because they never developed a practice of meditating on, reading and studying the Word. I have met some folks that have experienced salvation but they have remained babies in the Word. I have met a few that have had a head interest but not a heart knowledge. I have met some people that simply do not see the need to search the Scriptures and some are just lazy. I have been blessed with a desire to read the Bible. I have a determined heart to find the answers to life. I have made a deliberate choice and have not left it to circumstances. I have a disciplined motivation. Dedication has followed all the above. Therefore, drifting will not have a chance to create a problem for me.

How do I make the Bible my own? The Bible is a collection of life documents inspired by God. This statement alone should challenge me to make the Bible my own. I believe it is a God-breathed book. The two testaments go from creation to consummation, eternity past to eternity future. The Bible is the story of God, redeeming his chosen people for the promise of his glory. The Scriptures are God's self-revelation.

He reveals himself as the sovereign God of the universe who has chosen to create man and to make himself known to man. The Scriptures demonstrate the deadly effects in time and eternity of violating God's standard. There are 1,189 chapters in the Bible. Only four of them do not involve a fallen world. The Scriptures provide promises to those of us that trust God and seek to obey him. Divine blessing through faith will be abundant as I recognize God's standards and keep them. The Scriptures offer a substitute for me, one to die in my place. God's chosen substitute, the only one who qualified, was Jesus. God promises forgiveness through grace. Grace means that sin is not held against the sinner. The redemptive history started with a clear truth and will end with the same. The king was rejected and executed but he promised to come back in glory bringing judgment, resurrection and his kingdom for all who believe.

The Bible is becoming my own because it involves my story. I am a new creation in Jesus. I am being transformed into his image. I am his residence. It is an awesome responsibility. I am accountable to the Holy Spirit. He is also my enablement. I will not drift if I get the Bible-reading habit. This is my practice of making the Bible my own. I read a passage of Scripture repeatedly until I understand its theme. It might involve a week on one portion. I saturate my mind with the text. This is followed with deciding what the Scripture means. I have learned to allow the Scripture to interpret itself. This is where cross references and concordances come in handy. I let the Bible speak for itself and take it literally. I need to understand it from its historical context. The question should be, "what is the original intent?" I need to be careful with the grammatical structure. What is the phrase saying to me? I have to compare Scriptures with Scriptures — no contradictions. The use of commentaries and other Bible analyses are interesting. Personal application is the goal in the study. When I open it to my life and practice it daily, it will become my own.

Drifting from God only brings misery. Constantly abiding in him is the key to successful discipleship. Recently I had the wonderful opportunity to assist a friend that was dying of lung cancer. I watched him going through several different stages of the death process. When the soul and spirit begin to leave the body, there are different experiences. I am so grateful to Jesus Christ that he intercedes in the process. As my friend continued in his relationship, fellowship and intimacy with the Savior, it seemed that the Holy Spirit traveled with him into eternity. As he reflected upon God's grace, he recited the growth development he had received. This practice provided a satisfying reliance. Confidence in God's presence increased renewal in my friend's sickness and entrance into heaven. A restful sense of spirit came over him as God prepared his journey.

26

What is My Reliable Resource?

How do I draw near to Jesus to prepare for heaven? It is through accepting Jesus as the reliable resource. The Bible says, "for the Word of God is quick, and active, and sharper than any two-edged sword, piercing even to the dividing asunder of soul and spirit, and of the joints and marrow and is a discerner of the thoughts and intents of the heart" (Hebrews 4:12). This Scripture emphasizes that the Word of God is not only saving, comforting, nourishing and healing, it is also a tool of judgment and execution. The Word of God is "quick" living. It brings life to me. It is the way to life. I cannot disregard his word. God's Word will always do that which he designed it to do. I must take it seriously. It has transformed my life. In trusting in Jesus Christ as my Savior, he has made a new creation out of me (2 Corinthians 10:17). The Bible works. Why not try it out? It may surprise you. For me, every day it brings life to my daily experience. I cannot do anything without it. The word, "saving," means to rescue. I have been redeemed by God the Father, God the Son and God the Holy Spirit.

The Word of God is "active" and comforting. It is full of power and is efficient. It cannot be separated from God's person. Out of his words are "the issues of life" (John 6:3). As I face life's difficult issues, I am comforted with the fact that God is superior, sovereign and sufficient. Today with no absolutes, no guarantees, no standards and no moral uprightness, I still can be confident with the Scripture working in my life. As I mix it with faith, I will live abundantly (John 10:10). The word "comforting" means to console. I definitely have reassurance in life because God gives the support. In any affliction, I can find relief because God provides it.

The Word of God is "sharp" nourishment. If I believe the Word, it will bring life to my soul. If I reject it, I will receive death — eternal separation from God. The Bible is effective. It lays bare the soul of men. It is not only something to be studied, not only something to be read, not only something to be written about, it is something to do. The word "nourishing," refers to food. It is necessary for life, health and growth. It will strengthen and build me up. It provides the means to keep me alive.

The Word of God is "piercing" healing. It is able to penetrate my very being. God knows my innermost heart condition. Transparency is easy for God. He can distinguish between my emotions and will. He can see the soul and spirit. He gets right into the deepest human nature. He cuts through the most secret recesses of the spirit life. Joints and marrow are no problem for him. He can test my earthly life and my spiritual existence. He scrutinizes my true desires and intentions. He knows me. The word "healing," means mending. He is able to help me become sound in my growth pattern and he provides the process to obtain spiritual development.

The Word of God is "able to judge" discerning. God's Word is the perfect discerner. It not only analyzes all the facts perfectly but all motives, intentions and beliefs as well. Any disguises will not manage to deceive him. His word will make no mistakes. My real person will be seen. The word "judge" means to wisely make an opinion on a certain circumstance. He is the authority on discernment. No mistake on his part. The conclusions are honesty, fairness, just and merciful.

The Word of God is able to "execute" intents. I cannot evade God's compelling eyes. There is no escape. Nothing is concealed from God's eyes. There is no place to run or hide. I am naked before my maker. In that nakedness, I am made strong. Communion with God is possible through the blood of Jesus. The word "execute" means to perform a technical skill. It is the process and style of accomplishing something.

The Word of God is able to bring satisfaction, completeness, contentment, focus and rest. I am thankful for the Bible. It provides wisdom and discernment for my daily needs. It puts me into an accountability position. It provides confidence and encouragement. I cannot do without it. It is my reliable resource. It is a 'must' to get the Bible reading habit.

I love books and have many in my library. They are my tools. I have discovered knowledge, wisdom, discernment, understanding, motivation and desire. The list can continue on for a long time. The Bible is my life source. It gets me up in the morning and carries me through the day and puts me to bed at night. It helps me in perplexed times, uncertainties, weariness and times of contentment, happiness and joy. It is actually a shot into my bloodstream to keep me going. I hope I will be able to comprehend and understand it. Reflecting upon it gives me delight. Reciting it provides my enablement. My reliance in it provides daily strength. My renewal is through practicing it. My rest is the end product of it.

How Do I Rest in Jesus?

How do I draw near to Jesus to prepare for heaven? It is through accepting Jesus' peaceful rest. The Bible says, "Today, hear his voice (v.7), enter into rest through belief (v.3), earnestly enter into that rest" (Hebrews 4:1-10). In the Scriptures, we have the peace of God becoming a part of living and dying. We have the meaning of the promised land given to Israel and the rest of God after he completed the creation.

Resting refers to an attitude and state of peace in regards to the whole being. God is saying, I offer you the promise of rest, take advantage of it and do not fear your circumstances. Accept it as a challenge and enter into my peaceful rest. I have found it to be a necessary, refreshing quiet response when anxiety attacks the mind, when weariness has entered the body, when uncertainty has stressed the soul and when a spiritual calm is insecure. Tranquility and solitude integrated with listening to God, believing in God and acting on God's promise of rest can become reality when applied.

I am learning slowly to practice God's promise of rest. His superiority, sovereignty and sufficiency will prevail on my behalf. It starts with these words "let us therefore fear" (v.1). This fear is not which makes me run away from the task nor the fear which paralyzes. It is a fear of respect. It is the fear which makes me reach out for the promise of rest in my uncertain and my certain circumstances.

How do I experience the needed rest? "Today, hear his voice." The word, today is my challenge to respond. The promise is open today not tomorrow. It may not last forever. The promise can be missed. He says, "here and now through faith enter into the very rest of God." He says " hear my voice." There are many different kinds of hearing in this world. There is indifferent, cynical, disinterested, skeptical and eager hearing. Let's dominate the heart and head with an eager listening response. This will produce the decision to enter into rest through belief. Believing secures the enjoyment of God's rest. I can be refreshed because God is reliable. He will keep his promises. No matter how difficult life may be at times, he will come through. He is bigger than the problem I face. He is the solution. I have to listen to his voice and do something about what he says. Faith is "forsaking all I trust him." It is a decision to mix his Word with daily commitment.

Finally he says "earnestly enter into that rest." I have to give diligence to my quest for rest. It is a life of obedience not disobedience. It is not self-effort. My deep desire is to seek God's rest. I have to be spiritually engaged. "And the spirit of the Lord will come upon thee" (1 Samuel 10:6). "I will put my spirit within you and cause you to walk in my statutes and you shall keep my judgments and do them…I will be your God" (Ezekiel 36:26-28). "A new heart I will give you and a new spirit" (v.26). Praise God he provides the rest and makes the difference. Experience his promise of rest. I do not have to labor for it. I just ask for it, believe it, act upon it and be restored by it. Now it is up to you to be spiritually engaged. It really works. Focus on the creator, not the creation. He will give the needed rest. It is the work of the indwelling Holy Spirit.

As a visitation pastor, I have found myself in a hospice-ministry-dwelling place several times. The facilities and care are excellent. The staff that I have encountered is knowledgeable and sensitive to the needs. As I reflected upon dying, I found that it is very flexible. It arrives on the doorstep in many different ways. Separating the spirit from the physical body is a process. Reciting God's Word in "seeking his kingdom" (Matthew 6:33) in life and death will produce peace. Sometimes fear and resistance take place. Sometimes unfinished business has to take place. Learning to rely on Christ will help make the withdrawal from the world possible. Deliverance through his promise of rest will be obtained even if during death, disorientation may take place. Physical change will take place, a surge of energy might appear, restlessness, congestion and irregular breathing may occur, but the Holy Spirit will continue with my spirit and bring about restoration and rest. Thank God for his presence.

Who Is My Supreme Mediator?

How do I draw near to Jesus to prepare for heaven? It is through accepting Jesus as the mediator. "We have a great high priest who has passed through the heavens, Jesus the Son of God, let us hold fast our confessor" (Hebrews 4:14). A priest represents God before the people and the people before God. In the text, Jesus made a one-time perfect sacrifice on the cross. In chapter 1, he is seen as the one who has made purification of sins (1:3). In chapter 2, he is merciful and faithful (2:17). In chapter 3, he is the high priest in confession (3:1). Chapters 7-9, the focus is almost exclusive in Jesus' priesthood. When he says "passed through the heavens," it involves the atmosphere, outer space and the third heaven, God's abode (2 Corinthians 12:2-4). Jesus went to where God himself dwells. He sat down for all eternity at the Father's right hand (Hebrews 1:3).

By faith, I am able to enter directly into God's presence. When I come to God on his terms, I have access to him. Through Jesus Christ, my supreme mediator, I have been reconciled to God. His sacrifice was effective and final. The essential idea of the priesthood is found in Numbers 16:5. Three elements are involved: being set apart for Jehovah as his own, being holy, and being allowed to come near. Jesus Christ is my priest and mediator. Jesus has provided reconciliation. He represents God to man (2 Corinthians 5:18-20). There is no human merit involved. Jesus is my perfect priest-mediator because he is God-man. He not only had all the feelings of love, concern, disappointment, grief and frustration but he had much greater love, infinitely more sensitive concerns, infinitely higher standards of righteousness and perfect awareness of the evil and dangers of sin. He can sympathize with my weaknesses and yet he truly is divine.

The supreme mediator has sent me a comforter-helper (John 14:17). His name is called the Holy Spirit, the third person of the Trinity. The Holy Spirit is not an impersonal power or energy or influence. He is my comforter. He shall teach all things. His personal actions involve reproving, guiding, hearing, speaking, showing me through glorifying Christ and sharing the truth of Christ.

The Spirit dwells in me as my comforter helper. He knows my griefs, burdens, struggles, anxieties and fears. In his infinite wisdom, he knows how to apply grace. He makes me holy; "sanctify them through thy truth" (John 17:17). He cleanses from sin and sets me apart to God in love. He knows my unique nature, my weaknesses, my temptations and my place in the kingdom.

I must live in the conscious awareness of his indwelling presence. He is in me day and night in private life as well as public life. How does he work? His name spirit means 'breath' (Genesis 1:2; Ezekiel 37:14; John 14:26, 20:22). He is the breath of God. The Scriptures are God- breathed. The Bible is a product of God and will provide knowledge. He has breathed into me the breath of life. He is the source of all physical life in nature, whether plant, animal or human (Psalm 104:13). He has breathed into me the spiritual life. The new breath is God breathing his breath into me. He causes conviction. He has breathed into me his presence. He penetrates into the deepest inmost parts of my being (John 16:7). Intimate fellowship is the result.

He has breathed into me his power. Nothing is impossible (Luke 1:37) because he has the ultimate power (John 1:35). He has breathed into me a mystery (John 3:8). His ways are deep and wonderful. I marvel at his work and worship Jesus Christ with depth. Even when I do not comprehend, I marvel at his enablement.

As I reflect on the fact that Jesus is my supreme mediator, I have to bend my knee in humble reverence. As I study God's Word and recite its truths and principles, I have come to the conclusion that I need only one priest-mediator and that is Jesus Christ. This has caused a developing reliance. It has also brought deliverance from sin and acceptance by God the Father. God has chosen me, the Son has purchased me and the Holy Spirit has sealed me. Renewal and rest have become a part of my life because Jesus Christ is my Savior-Lord and priest-mediator.

How Do I Mature in My Faith?

How do I draw near to Jesus to prepare for heaven? It is through accepting the challenge to grow in faith. The Bible says, "Your ears have become dull" (Hebrews 5:11-14). The word 'dull' is interesting. It means a slow-moving mind. It means understanding is difficult. It means hearing is not clear. It can mean being forgetful. It is strong language and describes the nature of the person that is like a stone. It all comes down to thinking with a lazy mind. God wants me to mature. I cannot stay at a baby level of drinking the milk of the Word. I must pursue the solid food.

There are many Christians that refuse to grow up. There are many that neglect God's Word. There are many that are content. There is no interest in developing. There are many grown men and women that remain on the milk of the word. They refuse any opportunity to advance. Childhood behavior can be a result of lack of learning and applying the truth. Growth is necessary. The overall passage in Hebrews 5:11 — 6:12 deals with spiritual maturity. Dullness is gradual. They might have been stirred, moved and open at one time. I think the problem is that they have certain facts in a superficial way but the truth does not have them. They do not comprehend the fundamentals. I worked with a seminarian at one time and he was always talking theology. He sounded like a textbook and I thought he was interesting at times. I kept wondering when he arrived on the church door step or in the community, how he was going to communicate his faith. Then I thought about the possibility that maybe he only knows the facts and has a lot of knowledge, but he never allowed the 'Word' to enter his heart. Head knowledge is not enough. Heart infiltration must take place. Maturity will display discernment about what is right and wrong, true and false, helpful and harmful, and righteous and unrighteous.

How do I move from a dull mind to an alert mind? I am so thankful to the Lord Jesus Christ that I have a deep love for his Word. In my preaching ministry, I have been motivated to keep in the 'Word.' I did not dare not to be active in it. It has been a resource for what I was compelled to do.

In my devotional ministry, it has driven me to find spiritual solutions. My personal and public concerns have always brought me to the Scriptures. I do not know if it has been a habit-forming issue. I do not know if it has been a love-developing process. I do not know if it has been an inner-spiritual involvement or a psychological necessity. As I think about it, all of the above have attributed to my intimate consultation in the Word.

The dull mind will not happen if I keep an unbroken contact with Christ in a union of intimate love. The word 'abide' means simply to remain, to stay, to continue and to cling to (John 15). Do not allow anything to break that intimate union. Keep constantly depending on him. I can live with confidence because Jesus is the genuine vine. My life blood comes from Jesus. I must get rid of the dead branches. Life is too short to live with a 'dull' mind. All alternatives must be destroyed. Do not allow anything to come between the intimate union. I love the statement "abide in me and I in you" (John 15:4). Fruitfulness will be seen because he is working in me. Reflecting upon his mind will become a common reaction to life. My discipleship is evident of his abiding in me.

How do I keep constantly dependent on him? It is not hard once the process is generated. It becomes a natural process. Keep believing in his Word. Abiding in Christ and believing his word are interwoven. The command calls for time and responsibility. Take God at his Word. Commit and entrust your very being to it.

Keep obeying his Word. A life in Christ will be characterized by obedience. There is no exception to this. This involves yieldedness to him. Keep clinging to his Word. Remaining in his Word requires discipline. Pruning is necessary.

Real growth must take place. Let the trimming work take place. It is hard at times but worth it.

Keep praying in his Word. Be mindful that praying can be done in his will. It is based upon a continual conscious relationship with Christ. The Holy Spirit will convict, instruct and guide. This takes place through his Word. He will produce fruit in me when I abide in him and he abides in me. My desire is to be intimate with Jesus and not allow dullness to take place. If I get off the path, he will bring me back on it.

In my visitation ministry, I have been involved with several people that are in hospice care. This means they are preparing for their exit from this earth. Their spirit and soul are prepared to leave their earthly bodies and receive a heavenly one. As I reflect upon each soul, I have been challenged to become intimate with Jesus. Loving Jesus and walking close will prepare me for my journey. Reciting the word of God provides counsel and comfort. Confidence can be experienced because the Holy Spirit walks with the individual. Maturity and confidence are received through believing, obeying, clinging and praying. Reliance on the Creator-Savior is easy when I remain in Christ. I receive his strength every day. Renewal is needed and it is received because I have learned to rest in him.

30

What Does it Mean to Be a Partaker of the Holy Ghost?

How do I draw near to Jesus to prepare for heaven? It is through accepting the helper that Jesus has sent. The Bible says, they "were made partakers of the Holy Ghost" (Hebrews 6:4). The word 'partaker' in this passage has to do with association, not possession. It has to do with sharing a common event. In Hebrews 6:4, it refers to anyone who has been where the Holy Spirit has been ministering. Most of the multitude whom Jesus miraculously healed and fed partook of the Holy Spirit's power and blessings, but they did not have his indwelling. They only tasted the truth but did not entirely accept it into their lives.

As I meditated over this Scripture, I did not want to go half the way but to entirely embrace the Holy Spirit in my life. The phrase "the good Word of God" (Hebrews 6:5) led the way for me. I wanted to not only taste the Word but to actually digest it. His words became for me a joy and the delight of my heart (Jeremiah 15:16). I will receive a blessing from God because I have become "a partaker of the divine nature" (2 Peter 1:4). Through salvation in Jesus Christ, I am able to receive the indwelling Holy Spirit. The word 'partakers' in this passage emphasizes possession. Being born spiritually is a birth given by the Holy Spirit (John 3:6). "It is the spirit who gives this new life" (John 6:63). It is a gift from God through Jesus Christ (Romans 6:23). Judgment hangs over the human race. It involves physical, spiritual and eternal death. In his unregenerated condition, a person is alienated from God in this life and after death, this alienation continues in a place of everlasting punishment (Matthew 25:44). It is the spirit that brings eternal life (John 6:63).

As a believer in Christ, I have become a "partaker of the divine nature" (2 Peter 1:4). To experience the fullness of the comforter, I have to yield myself to him. This means that I have to place myself under his influence and control. I have to learn to submit to the leading of the indwelling Holy Spirit (Ephesians 5:18). It is a keep-being-filled decision.

How do I live every day with the Holy Spirit's presence? I must be conscious of following Jesus example and doing his will. I have to cooperate with the Holy Spirit in glorifying Christ. I have to have a sincere heart to be more like Christ (Philippians 3:10-14). I have to purify myself from sin (I John 3:2,3). I will be prepared for death by looking forward to being with Christ (2 Corinthians 5:8).

How do I live every day with the Holy Spirit's presence? I love being in his Word (2 Timothy 3:16,17). I am listening to what he has to say. I read it, study it, obey it and reflect upon it. It is my resource for living. It has proven that it is profitable. God says, "Let the word of Christ dwell in you" (Ephesians 5:19,20). I am being equipped through it. It takes commitment, discipline and the decision of faith.

Do I live every day with the Holy Spirit's presence? It is essential to continuously allow the Holy Spirit to fill me. I have to have an attitude of dependence. I am under the rule of Christ (Colossians 3:15-4:16; Ephesians 5:18-6:9). I am learning to allow Christ to dominate me. I am under the authority of the Bible. It tells me what to think and do. I have to practice confession. It is required for fellowship with the Almighty. Sharing love as a representative of Christ is necessary.

Do I live every day with the Holy Spirit's presence? If I have made the decision of faith in Jesus Christ, if I have been dominated by his Word and if I have been dependent on the Holy Spirit, I can live with confidence. God will do his part. This is an absolute. I must do my part. I can live with assurance that I am filled with the Holy Spirit. The evidence can be seen. It can be discovered in the deep joyful fellowship I have with Jesus and fellow believers. Mutual exhortation will provide peace, gratitude and obedience. It is evident in my sincere heart. I sing with grace in my heart to the Lord. The heart opens up the way to a sweet melody. I am also thankful. Gratitude will abound. Being thankful for everything and counting my blessings will do away with bad circumstances and hurtful experiences. They are pushed off the shelf through the concentration on the blessings. The spirit-filled life is evident through a reverent submission. A servant's heart is already seen. Humbleness replaces a proud heart. Gentleness replaces an aggressive heart. Meekness replaces a self-assertive heart. My challenge is to keep being filled and then I will be assured of the Holy Spirit's (my helper) presence.

As I reflect on the indwelling of the Holy Spirit, I have reviewed in my mind my confession of faith (Romans 10:9,10). At seven years of age, I believed in Jesus Christ as my Savior. Now after nearly seventy years, I am a witness of that indwelling. In reciting his Word and obeying that Word, I ask for the Holy Spirit's filling every day (Ephesians 6:18). When I served at the Kalamazoo Gospel Mission as their Director of Discipleship, I developed the habit to ask the Lord to fill me because of necessity. I never knew what would happen with the addictive fellows that I worked with. My reliance in the Lord deepened as I learned to walk daily with him. Every day would start with him and end with him. I have experienced the fulfillment of his promises when I would claim them through his authority. When I failed, and I have many times, I would be renewed through his grace. I am so thankful for his forgiveness, mercy and cleansing. I am learning to rest in his indwelling presence and to be filled daily. It is an exciting life. Glory to his name!

31

How Do I Build Relationships?

How do I draw near to Jesus to prepare for heaven? It is through making a decision to develop a relationship with him. The Bible says, "…he is able to save forever those who draw near to God through him, since he always lives to make intercession for them" (Hebrews 7:25). His enablement and intercession requires drawing near to him. This requires building a solid relationship. This text contains the whole essence of the gospel. Salvation is the main theme of the entire Bible. His salvation is secure. It is forever. It is complete and perfect. Jesus Christ is able to save eternally and completely. He is divine. This makes my salvation in him permanent. The phrase 'he is able' provides the power. I am writing about something that is absolute. Jesus is not only able to save, but he is the only one able to save. He is the only one who has the power (Acts 4:12). Through Jesus Christ, I am delivered from sin. This qualifies me to draw near to God. In the present tense, I am freed from sin's power. In the future tense, I shall be freed from sin's presence. Faith in Jesus Christ is the qualification to draw near (John 6:37). A perpetual intercession is active for me through Jesus Christ (Jude 3:4). He provides cleansing and a blameless life.

Drawing near involves sacrifice — am I taking a stand for Christ?
What do I have to surrender — self, time, money, will, etc.?

Drawing near involves superiority — am I living in his authority?
What do I have to understand — Christ's humanity, deity, awesomeness, enablement?

Drawing near involves selflessness — am I growing in grace?
What part does crucifying self, obtaining favor of God, receiving blessings have?

Drawing near involves servanthood — am I a genuine example?
What does it mean to be a bond slave?

Drawing near involves sinfulness — am I experiencing cleansing?
Have I become sensitive to bad behavior?

Drawing near involves sufficiency — am I victorious?
Have I learned to let go of self and yield completely?

Drawing near to Jesus will produce a restful spirit.
Have I experienced this rest?

"Whatsoever you do, do it heartily, as to the Lord and not unto men" (Colossians 3:23).

32

What Are Some Promises to Practice in Everyday Living?

How do I draw near to Jesus to prepare for heaven? It is through accepting the promises provided by Jesus. The Bible says, "This is the covenant that I will make with them after those days, saith the Lord, I will put my laws into their heart and in their minds will I write them; and their sins and iniquities will I remember no more…after you have done the will of God, ye might receive the promise" (Hebrews 10:16,17, 35-36).

The new covenant was not a new revelation but the fulfillment of an old one (Jeremiah 31:33,34). When I speak of the covenant, it refers to the covenant of the law with all its outward institutions and ritualistic services. The new covenant refers to grace that existed from the first. The word 'covenant' is applied to various transactions between God and man and between man and his fellow-men. It is a promise on the part of God to arrange his providences for the welfare of those who should render him obedience. Redeeming grace finds its source in the will of God. It was accomplished in the death of Christ. It was ratified by Christ sitting at God's right hand. It provides assurance in the witness of the Holy Spirit. The old covenant provided the repeated legal sacrifices. The new covenant provides one sacrifice in Jesus Christ. It is complete in him. Jesus is the living way to the presence of God. He is the bridge between man and God. He introduces me to God's very presence. Only Jesus can really cleanse me. It is not an external purification but an inner cleansing of the thoughts and desires. It is an honest response to the statement "You're Christ to me."

To experience the "You're Christ to me" example, I have to put his promises into action. I began reflecting upon the promise in the book of Hebrews. The challenge was to recite them and rely upon them. This brought renewal and rest. I am actually putting Hebrews 4:1-3 into reality. It says "the word preached did not profit them, not being mixed with faith." God has many blessings for his people. There is the blessing of salvation and the blessing of victory through obedient service to him. Am I willing to pay the price? How do I accomplish the blessings in my life? The answer is when I face the claims of Christ and determine by his grace to forsake everything which is displeasing to him. Salvation is free but victory demands work (Hebrews 4:11). The word 'work' is spelled with these letters; D-i-s-c-i-p-l-e-s-h-i-p. The word 'disciple' comes from the same root as the word 'discipline.' I have to learn that there is a price attached to following Jesus. It takes full surrender which involves strength, maturity, conviction, passion, bravery, dedication and faithfulness. If I do not process these characteristics, I will be disappointed, disillusioned, disarmed, discouraged and disqualified.

In God's covenant promise, I have a great sympathizing High Priest in heaven, I have an infallible Holy Spirit within and at the end of the way, I have a special reward. "For if we suffer with him we shall also reign with him." I pray that I will be the example of the statement, "You're Christ to me" and I will be if I mix the Word with faith. Here are some promises to start with found in my study of Hebrews:

Promise of Confidence	Hebrews 3:14
Promise of Discernment	Hebrews 4:12
Promise of Rest	Hebrews 8:8-10
Promise of Help	Hebrews 4:15,16
Promise of Encouragement	Hebrews 6:14,15
Promise of Endurance	Hebrews 10:23
Promise of Contentment	Hebrews 13:5

What is Faith?

"How do I draw near to Jesus to prepare for heaven?" It is through accepting the exercise of faith in Jesus. I like reading God's Word. Sometimes I read only a verse or two at a time. I listen to the impression it makes upon my spirit. My soul reacts with delight and talks to God through prayer. Faith requires thinking and illumination from the Holy Spirit. I need to know the meaning of faith and how to live victoriously with it. It starts with God speaking, "let us run with patience the race that is set before us. Looking unto Jesus the author and finisher of our faith" (Hebrews 12:1,2). The theme of Hebrews is a solemn warning against coming short of victory and encouragement to press on in spite of all my difficulties. Faith is the challenge. I remember in my childhood I learned a broad meaning of the word faith, "forsaking all I trust him." I want to build on its meaning. Remember that willful sinning, deliberate and continued disobedience and failure to judge known sin may result in "falling away." This results in God's judgment with only one purpose in mind - that of correction, not damnation.

I can have victory through faith. Victory implies a battle. Salvation is free, but victory means sacrifice. To win the race requires discipline. To experience victory, I have to understand faith. Conquering faith is what I am interested in. My childhood faith was easy. I took God at his Word. In my uncertainties in adult life, I have to do the same thing. I believe the unreasonable, the impossible and the unexplainable, because someone else in whom I have absolute confidence has said it was so. Upon his Word, I believe it without asking any further proof (Hebrews 11:1-3).

I accept the truth simply upon the word of someone else and without proof or any other evidence. It is believing what I cannot see, hear, feel, taste, smell or understand. It is confidence in another. Who do I trust? My belief in God is based upon the record of his Word. This is backed up by an eternity of faithfulness. No one who has ever put his trust in him has ever been lost or disappointed (1 John 5:9,10). I think it all goes back to Genesis 1:1. The natural man wants to reason out the origin of the universe and come up with a thousand speculations. The believer rests upon the simple statement of God. "In the beginning God created the heaven and the earth." God does not stop to explain. He is not obliged to satisfy my curiosity or to stoop to satisfy my mental concerns. He is absolute, final and true. This first verse of the Bible is the first example of faith. If I can believe that he spoke everything into existence and that he has no beginning or end, I can believe anything else he has to say. I can believe all the miracles: that he could become man and be God, that he prepared for my redemption, that his blood can cleanse me and that he is the author of faith and its authority.

The victory of faith is won through sacrifice. It is a battle and will cause wounds, scars and disappointments but in the end will be a glorious crown of victory. He requires me to surrender for service, to separate myself from the world, to abstain from sinful pleasures and to refuse to compromise with evil (Romans 12:2).

I absolutely need to know how to grow in faith since it is the key to living eternally. How do I live victoriously on a daily basis on my route to heaven? I have learned that worship starts the faith process. I must start with the Lamb of God. The foundation is in my salvation in Jesus Christ. He is the giver of faith. He provides the direction, guidance, authority and confidence. Religious activities are not the means. It is through my daily devotion to him (John 4:23) and relationship development. My worship will take me from the present to eternity and from eternity to an unending life with Christ. It will become a Holy-Spirit-stimulated vitality. True worhip requires me to approach God with my whole person. It is a love for God in gratitude for what he has done.

I have to experience an intimate relationship with God. My invisible part (spirit) must meet with God. My entire being is activated through love (Matthew 22:37,38). To understand faith requires God-consciousness. I initiate God-consciousness through praying, praising, reading the Bible, thoughtful meditations, etc. Faith will grow when I make the choice to be sensitive to God's will. I have to practice the presence of God. My union with Jesus Christ will establish a reliant trust and reverent worship.

The faith process starts with worship and will continue with a walk that glorifies Jesus Christ. I have to ask myself the question, "how deep is my fellowship with Jesus?" My developing communion with Jesus Christ begins by recognizing his residence in me. At the same time, my faith will grow because the foundation is sound. The divine genius of the Scriptures, the Holy Spirit, is my indwelling helper and counselor. A change has taken place because I have made a confession of faith (Romans 10:9,10). With that confession, the Holy Spirit dwells in me (Romans 8:9). I have a tremendous responsibility: will Christ be magnified in my body? The top priority is always to die to self. Yielding to God's will and dedication to Jesus as Lord is necessary. His indwelling presence is not in my imagination but the real thing.

The divine transformation will take place when I answer the question, what does it mean to be Christ-centered? Jesus says give me your body and your mind. I have to learn to respond to Jesus' demands. He is the dominate influence in my life. Applied Christianity is spiritual transformation. This involves sound doctrine, renewing of the mind, behavioral change and a willing heart.

The divine transformation will lead to the divine will. God will work his will in me. He is shaping me into the image of his son. Each day belongs to him and I must surrender all to him. His will is that I understand that the mind controls the body and the will controls the mind and the Spirit leads the way. I have to learn to just let go of self and let God do it. He will accomplish his will (Romans 12:1,2).

The faith process involves sincere worship, it involves a surrendered walk and sacrificial work. My work ethic is based upon eternity. "Work for the night is coming" (John 9:4). This phrase has led the way to many projects. Faith has opened the door. When worship has the proper motivation, it will prepare me to have the correct mindset (Biblical spirituality). When my walk (behavior) is Christ-centered, it will prepare me to live out what I believe within. The faith process will be reflected in the work God has given me to do. The proclamation of the Word through music, ministry and mentoring have all been built upon each other. It has been a joyful experience to reflect on his work being accomplished. Victorious faith will continue with a restful spirit in my life as I worship with sincerity, as I walk in surrender and as I work sacrificially. The Old Testament heroes of faith like Abel, Enoch and Noah will be my example. "I will run the race with patience….looking unto Jesus the author and finisher of my faith" (Hebrews 2:1-3).

34

Who is Watching Me?

How do I draw near to Jesus to prepare for heaven? It is through accepting the responsibility of being Christ-like. The Bible says, "Wherefore seeing we also are compassed about with so great a cloud of witnesses, let us aside every weight and the sin which doth easily beset us and let us run with patience the race that is before us" (Hebrews 12:1). Let us study the text. Each word is important. "Wherefore" refers to the previous chapter. It is the roster of faithful heroes. I need to look at their trials and triumphs. I need to listen to their voices. Their testimony is worth following. In a broad sense, all believers and born again saints are touched in this text. The words "cloud of witnesses" emphasizes the heavenly saints. They are witnesses to God, not of us. They are examples, not onlookers. They have proved by their testimony and their witness that the life of faith is the only life to live. God helped them and he will help me. The same God who was their God is mine.

How should I respond? How can I please God? "Lay aside every weight" — these words mean that everything that would entangle my feet must be gotten rid of. It may not be bad and it may be innocent and harmless. It is whatever diverts my attention, whatever keeps me from running the race well. I do not need to carry excess baggage.

I must be sensitive to any hindrance that drives me away from God. My major focus should always be living a holy life set apart to Jesus Christ. Unbelief and doubt need to be erased from my life. Every day should be faced with the armor of God and living in victory. If I trip or stumble, I have to learn how to get up and keep running. "Run with patience" — perseverance is the word to practice in the Christian race. It is understanding God's patience and experiencing his enablement. Endurance is necessary in the trial. Keep at it no matter the circumstances or situations that may try to hinder.

"Looking unto Jesus" means to look away from all things and fix my eyes on Jesus with an earnest heart. Do not be preoccupied with self. Do not be distracted. Be filled with the Spirit. This command will place my focus on Jesus Christ alone. He is the author and perfector of faith. He is the supreme example of my faith. I cannot fail if I abide in Jesus because he is the originator and inventor of my faith. He is also in the process of perfecting it. He will complete it in my life. Jesus is the pre-eminent example of faith. He endured the cross and was victorious. My life is to glorify God by allowing his attributes to shine through me and by doing his will in everything. Jesus is my motivator. The Holy Spirit is my help and I do what I do to glorify God my heavenly Father, who is watching me.

When I first read my question, "who is watching me?" it made me nervous and uneasy. I reflected upon the theme in my study of Hebrews and became challenged. I live in a glass house and need to be aware that I should be a bright light shining for God's glory. I recited my text "so great cloud of witnesses" and was motivated to think that the saints of the past can possibly see me or perhaps these are witnesses to God, not me. They are excellent examples, not onlookers. The important issue is that I rely upon God through Jesus Christ and the illumination of the Holy Spirit. My focus has to be upon Jesus. He is deity and can see me because of who he is. A renewal of my heart and responsibility to my Lord places me in the humble position of submission. I rest on Jesus. My goal is to be a good example for Jesus. If I am alright before him, I will be alright in the face of others whether they accept the truth or not.

35

What is My Heavenly Citizenship Based Upon?

How do I draw near to Jesus to prepare for heaven? My citizenship in heaven is based upon my relationship with Jesus Christ. I enjoy taking the text of the Scriptures apart. It is fun to analyze and examine life producing exhortations. Every word can change life experiences. I am going to take God breathed words to declare my heavenly citizenship. The text is Hebrews 13:20-21:

"May the God of peace" refers to the fact that he is the author and dispenser of peace. I can trust my life to him. Peace is a result of that trust. God is the authority. He is my creator, redeemer and Lord. I have peace with God and peace of God in my life.

The words "Blood of the eternal covenant" emphasizes that the blood of Christ shed on the cross secures God's promises for those who believe. I can rest in my decision of faith to rely on his word.

"Brought back from the dead" are powerful words. Jesus Christ Is life because he conquered death. Enablement is mine through the power of the resurrection. If I believe, I have access to the power of God.

"Our Lord Jesus" is sovereign and Savior. I can enjoy my life in Christ because he is in control. He is my "Great Shepherd. " He is the best caregiver. I am thankful that God provides the necessary training and gifts. He will equip me with everything good. He equips me for doing his will. Under the new covenant, he provides power to do his will and reveals his will. The key is to will my will to him.

The words "through Jesus Christ" emphasize development. It involves sacrifice, obedience, discipline, fellowship and trust. The text ends with "to whom be glory forever and ever, Amen."

Jesus Christ is the object of glory. I have been invited to participate in God's plan to bring honor to Jesus. My heavenly Father does the cultivating, my Savior is the mediator and the Holy Spirit gives the moment by moment enablement. "It is and shall be" are the secure words that give the final stamp of approval for my citizenship.

Sources

Barnes, Albert — Matthew and Mark — Baker Book House 1956

Barnes, Albert — Luke and John — Baker Book House

Berry, George R — The Interlinear — Greek English New Testament, Zondervan Publishing House

Halley, Henry — Bible Handbook — Chicago, Illinois 1927

Martin, Alfred — John-Life Through Believing, Moody Press 1959

Tenney, Merrill C. — John, the Gospel of Belief, Wm Eerdman's Publishing Company 1953

Unger and Merrill F — Unger's Bible Dictionary, Moody Press 1957

Wuest, Kenneth S — The Gospels,
Wm Eerdman's Publishing Company 1955

Falwell, Jerry — Liberty Bible Commentary,
The Old-Time Gospel Hour 1983

Wiersbee, Warren — Be Compassionate,
Chariot Victor 1988

Barclay, William — The Gospel of Luke,
Westminster Press 1956

Boice, James Montgomery — Foundations of the
Christian Faith, Intervarsity Press 1986

Evans, Tony — Our God is Awesome, Moody Press 1994

Geisler, Norman — Unshakable Foundations,
Bethany House 2001

Matthew, Victor — Daily Affirmation of Faith,
Notes 1980

Unknown, From The Heart — The Life Model 2010

Graham, Billy — Nearing Home, Thomas Nelson 2011

Stowell, Joseph M. — Eternity, Moody Press 1995

Jeremiah, David — When Your World Falls Apart, Thomas Nelson 2000

DeHaan, M.R — Hebrews, Zondervan Publishing House 1959

MacArthur, John — The MacArthur New Testament Commentary Hebrews, Moody Bible Institute 1983

All Scripture quotations are taken from the King James Version of the Bible. Thomas Nelson Incorporated, 1976

Acknowledgements

I appreciate all the people that God has used to influence me. Many of these thoughts have come to my memory over the past seventy-five years through sermon notes, lectures, conversations, meditations and reading. I have not knowingly withheld any significant reference from others in my devotional. To the best of my knowledge, all statements and information are true and correct and given credit. Everyone I have come in contact with should be given credit. The devotional is a constant source of strength, support and security for me and I hope for you.

www.ingramcontent.com/pod-product-compliance
Lightning Source LLC
Chambersburg PA
CBHW070103080526
44586CB00013B/1170